MASTERING THE AMERICAN ACCENT

Lisa Mojsin, M.A.

Director, Accurate English, Inc.

Los Angeles, CA

BARRON'S

Acknowledgments

This book is dedicated to my accent reduction students who came to the United States from all parts of the globe. Their drive to excel, passion for learning, amazing work ethic, and belief in the American dream have inspired me to write this book. In the words of Henry David Thoreau, "Go confidently in the direction of your dreams. Live the life you have imagined."

Thanks to all of the supportive and extremely professional people at Barron's: Dimitry Popow, my editor; Wayne Barr for seeking me out to write this book; and Veronica Douglas for her support.

I am enormously grateful to Lou Savage, "The Voice." His is the beautiful male voice on the recordings. He was also responsible for all of the expert audio engineering and audio editing. Thank you, Lou, for being such a perfectionist with the sound and insisting on fixing the audio "mistakes" I couldn't hear anyway.

I am also grateful for the contributions of Maryam Meghan, Jack Cumming, Katarina Matolek, Mauricio Sanchez, Sabrina Stoll, Sonya Kahn, Jennie Lo, Yvette Basica, Marc Basica, and Laura Tien.

Address all inquiries to:
Barron's Educational Series, Inc.
250 Wireless Boulevard
Hauppauge, NY 11788
www.barronseduc.com

ISBN-13: 978-0-7641-4185-0 (book only)
ISBN-10: 0-7641-4185-6 (book only)
ISBN-13: 978-0-7641-9582-2 (book & CD package)
ISBN-10: 0-7641-9582-4 (book & CD package)

Library of Congress Control Number 2008938576

Printed in the United States of America
9 8 7 6 5 4 3 2

Contents

Chapter 5: Syllable Stress 66

Chapter 6: Word Stress 78

Chapter 7: Intonation 95

Chapter 8: Sound Like a True Native Speaker 101

Chapter 9: Memorizing the Exceptions 119

Native Language Guide 127

Index 184

Introduction

This book will help non-native speakers of English learn to speak with an American accent.

Which American Accent Will This Book Teach Me?

You will learn to produce the standard American accent. Some people also call it "broadcaster English." It's the kind of standard, neutral speech that you hear on CNN and in educated circles. It's a non-regional American accent, meaning that people do not associate the dialect with any particular part of the United States. It is the accent most commonly associated with educated people in the American East, Midwest, and West.

How Should I Practice?

Listen to the recorded material over and over. You will hear words and sentences pronounced followed by a pause for you to repeat after the speaker. You may want to record yourself repeating so that you can compare your accent to the accents of the speakers on this audio. Then practice the new sounds in real-life situations.

There are numerous study tips throughout the book, both from the writer and from her many successful students who have greatly improved their American accent. For an individual professional analysis of your accent which will help you to study accent reduction more efficiently and tell you which sections of this book you should focus on most, please contact us at 1-800-871-1317 or visit our website at: *masteringtheamericanaccent.com*.

Chapter One

THE VOWEL SOUNDS

In this chapter you will learn how to accurately pronounce all of the main American English vowel sounds. The English alphabet has five vowels, *a, e, i, o* and *u,* but it has about 15 main vowel sounds. For some learners this is one of the most difficult aspects of American English to master. Speakers of languages with fewer vowel sounds are likely to speak English using only the same number of sounds that exist in their native language. Sometimes they do not even hear the distinction between certain sounds in English. Consequently, non-native speakers might pronounce "hill" and "heal" the same way. Similarly, the words *sell* and *sale,* or *cup, cop,* and *cap* may also sound the same when spoken by a non-native speaker.

Because there is not always a direct relationship between how a word is spelled and how it is pronounced, you should become familiar with the phonetic symbols that represent the sounds that you are learning. This way, you will be able to use your dictionary when you come across a word that contains a vowel sound that you don't know how to pronounce. Make sure you also become familiar with the phonetic symbols of your dictionary as they may be a bit different from the symbols that this book uses.

Main Vowel Sounds of American English

1. /i/	*read, heat, meet, seat, seen, feet*	Please <u>ea</u>t the m<u>ea</u>t and the ch<u>ee</u>se before you l<u>ea</u>ve.
2. /ɪ/	*in, bit, this, give, sister, will, city*	My s<u>i</u>ster L<u>i</u>nda w<u>i</u>ll l<u>i</u>ve <u>i</u>n the b<u>i</u>g c<u>i</u>ty.
3. /eɪ/	*late, gate, bait, fail, main, braid, wait*	J<u>a</u>ne's f<u>a</u>ce looks gr<u>ea</u>t for her <u>a</u>ge of <u>eigh</u>ty-<u>eigh</u>t.
4. /ɛ/	*let, get, end, any, fell, bread, men, said*	I w<u>e</u>nt to T<u>e</u>xas for my fri<u>e</u>nd's w<u>e</u>dding.
5. /æ/	*last, apple, add, can, answer, class*	The h<u>a</u>ndsome m<u>a</u>n lost his b<u>a</u>ggage <u>a</u>fter his tr<u>a</u>vels.
6. /ɑ/	*stop, lock, farm, want, army, possible, got*	J<u>o</u>hn is p<u>o</u>sitive that his c<u>a</u>r was p<u>a</u>rked in that l<u>o</u>t.
7. /ə/	*come, up, jump, but, does, love, money, about*	Your y<u>ou</u>nger br<u>o</u>ther d<u>oe</u>sn't tr<u>u</u>st <u>u</u>s, d<u>oe</u>s he?

8. /ɔ/	all, fall, author, also, applaud, thought, fought	Paula was doing laundry all day long.
9. /oʊ/	go, slow, so, those, post, moment, drove	Oh, no! Don't open the window, it's cold.
10. /ʊ/	look, took, put, foot, full, wolf, cookie	He would read the good book if he could.
11. /u/	cool, soup, moon, boot, tooth, move, true	Sue knew about the food in the room.
12. /ɚ/	her, work, sure, first, early, were, earn, occur	What were the first words that girl learned?
13. /aɪ/	time, nine, dry, high, style, five, China	I advise you to ride a bicycle in China.
14. /aʊ/	south, house, cow, found, down, town	He went out of the house for about an hour.
15. /ɔɪ/	oil, choice, moist, enjoy, avoid, voice	Let's avoid the annoying noise.

Production of Vowels

We categorize vowels as **front**, **middle**, or **back** depending on which part of the tongue is used to produce the sound. For example, /i/ is a front vowel because the front part of the tongue goes up in the front of the mouth, and /u/ is a back vowel because the back of the tongue goes up in the back of the mouth. We also categorize vowels as **high** or **low**. In high vowels, the tongue is pushed up high near the roof of the mouth as in /i/, and in low vowels, the tongue is flat down at the bottom of the mouth, as in /ae/.

Diphthongs consist of two different vowel sounds that are closely joined together and treated as one vowel. They are represented by two phonetic symbols. To create this sound, move your tongue smoothly from one vowel position to another. The following vowels are diphthongs: /eɪ/ as in *take*, /oʊ/ as in *boat*, /aɪ/ as in *time*, /aʊ/ as in *house*, and /ɔɪ/ as in *boy*.

You will now learn how to correctly pronounce each type of vowel. Refer to the diagrams below to help you better understand the correct tongue and lip positions for these various vowel sounds.

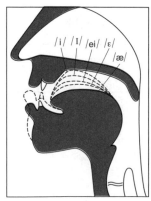

front

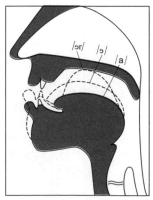

middle

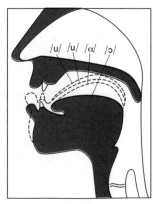

back

/i/ AS IN *MEET*

*A th**ie**f bel**ie**ves everybody st**ea**ls.*
E.W. Howe

Lips: Slightly smiling, tense, not rounded.
Tongue: Tense, high and far forward near the roof of the mouth.

Common Spelling Patterns for /i/

1. *ee*   *meet, feel, see, free*
2. *ea*   *team, reach, mean, sea*
3. *ie* and *ei*   *belief, piece, neither, receive*
4. final *e*   *me, we, she, he*
5. *e + consonant + e*   *these, Chinese, Peter*
6. final *y*   *city, duty, country, ability*
7. endings with *ique*   *unique, boutique, critique*

Word Pairs for Practice

1. deep sea
2. beans and cheese
3. severe heat
4. breathe deep
5. three meals
6. green leaves
7. extremely easy
8. sweet dreams
9. peaches and cream
10. speak Chinese

Practice Sentences

1. The employees agreed to meet at eight fifteen.
2. Don't keep the TV near the heater.
3. It's extremely easy to cheat when the teacher isn't here.
4. Please speak to Peter about the employee meeting.
5. Steve will reread the email before he leaves.

/ɪ/ AS IN *SIT*

***I**n the m**i**ddle of a d**i**fficulty lies opportun**i**ty.*
Albert Einstein

Lips: Slightly parted, relaxed.
Tongue: Relaxed, high, but not as high as for /i/. Sides of the tongue touch upper back teeth.

Common Spelling Patterns for /I/

1. *i* (most common)	*sit, give, this, dinner*
2. *ui*	*build, quit, quick, guilty*
3. *y* between two consonants	*system, gym, symbol, hymn*

exceptions:

been	in American English *been* is pronounced the same as *bin*, but in British English *been* sounds like *bean*.
women	sounds like *wimin* (the *o* is an /I/ sound)

Word Pairs for Practice

1. big city		6. fish and chips
2. innocent victim		7. trip to Italy
3. drink milk		8. spring picnic
4. children's film		9. this thing
5. simple living		10. winter wind

Practice Sentences

1. Kim will visit her big sister Linda in Virginia.
2. In the beginning it was difficult for Jim to quit drinking.
3. The Smiths invited him to an informal dinner.
4. This city has an interesting history.
5. When did Bill Clinton visit the Middle East?

Quick Review
Word Contrasts for /i/ Versus /I/

Make sure you don't pronounce these pairs of words the same.

	/i/	/I/		/i/	/I/
1.	leave	live	7.	beat	bit
2.	feel	fill	8.	steal	still
3.	least	list	9.	each	itch
4.	he's	his	10.	seek	sick
5.	sleep	slip	11.	feet	fit
6.	cheap	chip	12.	sheep	ship

Word Pairs for Practice

Make sure the two words in each pair are pronounced with different vowel sounds.

1. still sleepy
2. very interesting
3. feeling ill
4. it's easy
5. is he?

6. big deal
7. these things
8. Middle East
9. little meal
10. green pill

/eɪ/ AS IN *TAKE*

Take time for all things: great haste makes great waste.
Benjamin Franklin

Lips: Not rounded, relaxed.
Tongue: Tense, moves from the mid-high to high position.

Common Spelling Patterns for /ei/

1. *a* + consonant + *e*	*late, came, take, save*
2. *ai*	*rain, wait, pain, aim*
3. *ay*	*say, away, play, Monday*
4. *ey*	*they, survey, obey*
5. *eigh*	*weigh, eight, neighbor, freight*
6. *a*	
	less common:
	April, alien, angel

Word Pairs for Practice

1. the same day
2. stay away
3. escape from jail
4. take a break
5. stay the same

6. explain the situation
7. play baseball
8. eighty-eight
9. bake a cake
10. save the whales

Practice Sentences

1. She complained about her weight but ate the cake anyway.
2. Jake hates waiting for trains and planes.
3. It rains and hails in April and May.
4. I will stay in the game even though it's late.
5. My neighbor from Spain moved away today.

/ɛ/ AS IN *GET*

Every exit is an entry somewhere.
Tom Stoppard

Lips: Farther apart than for /eɪ/ and relaxed.
Tongue: Relaxed, mid-high position.

Common Spelling Patterns for /ɛ/

1. *e*   *get, end, next, general*
2. *ea*   *heavy, head, read, measure*

exceptions:
said, says again, against, any, many

 Warning: Common Mistake

The verb *say* is pronounced with the /ɛ/ sound in the past tense form and in the present tense form when it is followed by an *s*.

/eɪ/	/ɛ/
I s<u>ay</u>	I s<u>ai</u>d
	he s<u>ay</u>s

Word Pairs for Practice

1. presidential election
2. bend your legs
3. plenty of energy
4. remember the pledge
5. better friend
6. heavy metal
7. get better
8. elegant dress
9. next Wednesday
10. well read

Practice Sentences

1. Without some extra effort you will never excel.
2. Jenny and her friend had eggs for breakfast.
3. I expect this session to end at ten.
4. On the seventh of February the weather was wet.
5. I see my best friend Fred every seven days.

Quick Review
Word Contrasts for /ɛ/ Versus /eɪ/

Make sure you don't pronounce these pairs of words the same.

/ɛ/ and /eɪ/			/ɛ/ and /eɪ/	
1. pen	pain		5. tell	tail
2. sell	sail		6. Ed	aid
3. wet	wait		7. test	taste
4. west	waste		8. men	main

Word Pairs for Practice

Make sure the two words in each pair are pronounced with different vowel sounds.

1. less rain
2. taste test
3. neck pain
4. fell away
5. wet day
6. main men
7. great dress
8. headache

/æ/ AS IN *FAT*

He who laughs last laughs best.
American proverb

Lips: Open, not rounded.
Tongue: Lowest of all the front vowels. Flat on the floor of the mouth.

Common Spelling Patterns for /æ/

a	*hat, apple, man, answer*

Word Pairs for Practice

1. bad example
2. national anthem
3. back at the ranch
4. accurate answer
5. bad habit
6. practical plan
7. annual gathering
8. last chance
9. handsome actor
10. angry man

Practice Sentences

1. This is your last chance to give me an accurate answer.
2. Sam sat at the back of the math class.
3. Danny had a salad and a sandwich in the cafeteria.
4. Nancy has a bad attitude in her Spanish class.
5. Kathy would rather study acting at the national academy.

Quick Review
Word Contrasts for /ɛ/ Versus /æ/

Make sure you don't pronounce these pairs of words the same.

/ɛ/	/æ/		/ɛ/	/æ/
1. men	man	5.	guess	gas
2. said	sad	6.	slept	slapped
3. end	and	7.	head	had
4. then	than	8.	expensive	expansive

Word Pairs for Practice

Make sure the two words in each pair are pronounced with different vowel sounds: /ɛ/ or /æ/.

1. sad endings
2. less land
3. angry men
4. ten gallons
5. last exit
6. bad friend

/ɑ/ AS IN *FATHER*

Never go to a doctor whose office plants have died.
Erma Bombeck

Lips: Apart, as if you are yawning. Not rounded.
Tongue: Relaxed, flat at the floor of the mouth.

Common Spelling Patterns for /ɑ/

o	*hot, stop, modern, job*
a	*father, watch, dark, want*

Word Pairs for Practice

1. common problem
2. body shop
3. occupy the office
4. office politics
5. from top to bottom
6. logical response
7. hot topic
8. modern hospital
9. nonstop
10. sloppy job

Practice Sentences

1. Ronald is confident that he got the job.
2. Scott goes to a lot of rock concerts.
3. The doctor operated in the modern hospital.
4. Bob will probably lock the office.
5. He's got a lot of dollars in his pocket.

Quick Review
Word Contrasts for /æ/ Versus /ɑ/

Make sure you don't pronounce these pairs of words the same.

	/æ/	/ɑ/			/æ/	/ɑ/
1.	hat	hot		5.	cap	cop
2.	lack	lock		6.	add	odd
3.	sack	sock		7.	rack	rock
4.	sang	song		8.	tap	top

Word Pairs for Practice

Make sure the two words in each pair are pronounced with different vowel sounds: /æ/ or /ɑ/.

1. h<u>o</u>t p<u>a</u>n
2. m<u>a</u>n's j<u>o</u>b
3. t<u>o</u>p <u>a</u>nswer
4. g<u>o</u>t b<u>a</u>ck
5. b<u>a</u>d d<u>o</u>g
6. b<u>a</u>ck p<u>o</u>cket

Advice from a Successful Student

"During my drive to and from work, I always listen to audio books. The speaker's voice is usually very clear and not sloppy like the speech I sometimes hear on the street. I listen closely to the accent of the speaker and try to imitate it. I play back certain parts over and over again. The more I do this the better my accent gets."

Katarina Matolek, Croatia

/ə/ AS IN *FUN**

L<u>o</u>ve all, tr<u>u</u>st a few, do wrong to n<u>o</u>ne.
William Shakespeare

Lips: Completely relaxed, slightly parted.
Tongue: Relaxed, middle position.

Common Spelling Patterns for /ə/

u	*but, fun, summer, drunk*
o	*love, done, come, son*
ou	*cousin, country, enough*

---

*The IPA (International Phonetic Alphabet) symbol for the stressed vowel is /ʌ/ and for the unstressed vowel it is /ə/. They are basically the same sound. Throughout this book the /ə/ will be used for both. For further study of this reduced, neutral sound, refer to Chapter Five, which deals with syllable stress and reduced vowels.

CD 1
Track
33

Word Pairs for Practice

1. young son
2. jump up
3. fun in the sun
4. another subject
5. wonderful mother

6. under the rug
7. number one
8. undercover
9. enough money
10. Sunday Brunch

CD 1
Track
34

Practice Sentences

1. Your younger brother doesn't trust us.
2. What country does he come from?
3. I had another fun summer in London.
4. I don't have much stuff in the trunk of my truck.
5. I love the sunny summer months.

CD 1
Track
35

Quick Review

Word Contrasts for /ɑ/ Versus /ə/

Make sure you don't pronounce these pairs of words the same.

	/ɑ/	/ə/			/ɑ/	/ə/
1.	Don	done	5.	lock	luck
2.	shot	shut	6.	non	none
3.	fond	fund	7.	robber	rubber
4.	got	gut	8.	doll	dull

CD 1
Track
36

Word Pairs for Practice

Make sure the two words in each pair are pronounced with different vowel sounds: /ɑ/ or /ə/.

1. c**o**me **o**n
2. g**o**t l**u**cky
3. n**o**t en**ou**gh
4. c**o**st m**u**ch

5. f**u**n j**o**b
6. st**o**p r**u**nning
7. j**u**mp **o**n
8. g**u**nsh**o**t

CD 1
Track
37

/ɔ/ AS IN *SAW*

*Courage is the first of human q**ua**lities bec**au**se it is the q**ua**lity
which guarantees **a**ll the others.*
Winston Churchill

Lips: Apart, very slightly rounded, oval shape.
Tongue: Slightly tense, down near the floor of mouth.

Common Spelling Patterns for /ɔ/

aw	*saw, law, awful, awesome*
au	*author, August, applaud, audition*
al	*small, walk, tall, always*
ought	*bought, thought, fought*
aught	*daughter, caught*
o	*gone, off, long*

Word Pairs for Practice

1. pause in the hall
2. awful thought
3. water the lawn
4. talk until dawn
5. autumn in Austria
6. walk the dog
7. small talk
8. already exhausted
9. tall wall
10. caught the ball

Practice Sentences

1. The audience applauded even though the talk was awful.
2. His small daughter thought that Santa Claus would come in August.
3. I saw your mother-in-law in the mall.
4. He bought an automobile at the auction last fall.
5. This sauce is awesome, Paula!

Quick Review

Word Contrasts for /ə/ Versus /ɔ/

Make sure you don't pronounce these pairs of words the same.

	/ə/	/ɔ/		/ə/	/ɔ/
1.	cut	caught	5.	but	bought
2.	hull	hall	6.	sung	song
3.	done	dawn	7.	cuff	cough
4.	dug	dog	8.	flood	flawed

Word Pairs for Practice

Make sure the two words in each pair are pronounced with different vowel sounds: /ə/ or /ɔ/.

1. another dog
2. long month
3. much talk
4. bought lunch
5. coffee cup
6. small club

/oʊ/ AS IN *BOAT*

No bird soars too high if he soars with his own wings.
William Blake

Lips: Very rounded and tense.
Tongue: A bit tense, moves from mid to high position.

Common Spelling Patterns for /oʊ/	
o	*no, don't, home, only*
oa	*road, coat, boat*
ow	*own, slow, window*
ough	*though, although*

Word Pairs for Practice

1. phone home
2. own a home
3. almost over
4. open road
5. drove slowly
6. don't smoke
7. low profile
8. slow motion
9. old poem
10. golden bowl

Practice Sentences

1. We both hope it's going to snow.
2. Oh, no! Don't open the window! It's cold.
3. Do you want to go bowling or roller skating?
4. I chose a bowl of soup, potatoes, roast beef, and a soda.
5. I don't know if Joan smokes.

Quick Review

Word Contrasts for /ɑ, ɔ/ Versus /oʊ/

Make sure you don't pronounce these pairs of words the same. Please note that /ɑ/ and /ɔ/ sound almost the same, and therefore are both listed in the first column.

	/ɑ, ɔ/	/oʊ/		/ɑ, ɔ/	/oʊ/
1.	bought	boat	6.	caught	coat
2.	law	low	7.	walk	woke
3.	clause	close	8.	not	note
4.	odd	owed	9.	got	goat
5.	want	won't	10.	non	known

Word Pairs for Practice

Make sure the two words in each pair are pronounced with different vowel sounds: /ɑ, ɔ/ or /oʊ/

1. <u>o</u>ld l<u>a</u>w
2. n<u>o</u>t h<u>o</u>me
3. th<u>o</u>se d<u>o</u>gs
4. <u>o</u>dd b<u>oa</u>t
5. w<u>a</u>lk sl<u>ow</u>ly
6. <u>o</u>nly d<u>au</u>ghter

/ʊ/ AS IN *GOOD*

*Without words, without writing and without b**oo**ks there w**ou**ld*
*be no history, there c**ou**ld be no concept of humanity.*

Hermann Hesse

Lips: Very slightly rounded.
Tongue: Relaxed, back is raised, higher than for /oʊ/.

Common Spelling Patterns for /ʊ/

oo	*good, look, childhood, understood*
u	*push, full, pull, sugar*
ould	*would, could, should*
exception:	woman sounds like *"wumun"*

Word Pairs for Practice

1. good book
2. took a look
3. good looking
4. fully cooked
5. shook his foot
6. sugar cookie
7. push and pull
8. wool pullover
9. wooden hook
10. good childhood

Practice Sentences

1. Would you help me look for my book?
2. The sugar cookies taste good.
3. The butcher is a good cook.
4. He would read the book if he could.
5. Butch visited his old neighborhood in Brooklyn.

/u/ AS IN *TOO*

*If you could ch**oo**se one characteristic that would get you thr**ou**gh life,*
*ch**oo**se a sense of h**u**mor.*

Jennifer Jones

Lips: Tense, rounded, as if blowing a balloon.
Tongue: Slightly tense, high.

Common Spelling Patterns for /u/

oo	*too, food, school, tool*
ue	*true, blue, avenue*
o	*do, who, lose, prove*
ew	*new, blew, drew*
u	*super, rule, duty, student*

Word Pairs for Practice

1. too few
2. fruit juice
3. soup spoon
4. new suit
5. true value

6. blue shoes
7. new moon
8. suitable suitcase
9. two rooms
10. super cool

Practice Sentences

1. The new roof was installed in June.
2. I drink fruit juice and eat a lot of soup.
3. Your blue shoes are really cool.
4. I need proof that you're telling the truth.
5. The statue on the avenue is truly beautiful.

Quick Review

Vowel Contrasts for /ʊ/ Versus /u/

Make sure you don't pronounce these pairs of words the same.

	/ʊ/	/u/			/ʊ/	/u/
1.	full	fool		3.	pull	pool
2.	look	Luke		4.	stood	stewed

Word Pairs for Practice

Make sure the two words in each pair are pronounced with different vowel sounds: /ʊ/ or /u/.

1. good food
2. full room
3. cook stew

4. blue book
5. two cookies
6. too full

/ɚ/ AS IN *BIRD*

Life is uncertain. Eat dessert first.
Ernestine Ulmer

Lips: Slightly rounded.
Tongue: Tense, mid-level position. Tip is curled up a bit and pulled back.

Common Spelling Patterns for /ɚ/

er	*her, mercy, mother, winner*
ear	*heard, learn, earth*
ir	*first, girl, firm*
or	*doctor, word, worry*
ur	*occur, curtain, jury*
ure	*insecure, culture*
ar	*grammar, collar*

Word Pairs for Practice

1. first person
2. purple shirt
3. learn German
4. other world
5. serve dinner
6. third term
7. firm words
8. early bird
9. nervous girl
10. thirty-third

Practice Sentences

1. I will work during the third term.
2. They served turkey for dinner.
3. Her purple shirt is dirty.
4. She gave birth to a third girl.
5. It's not worth worrying about another birthday.

/aɪ/ AS IN *TIME*

We must use time wisely and forever realize that the time is always ripe to do right.
Nelson Mendela

Lips: Open, not rounded, closing a bit when moving to the /ɪ/ position.
Tongue: Relaxed, moves from flat to high position.

Common Spelling Patterns for /aɪ/

y	*fly, sky, apply, style*
i	*nice, kind, fine, sign*
igh	*light, fight, sight, night*
ie	*lie, tie, tried*

Word Pairs for Practice

1. lime pies
2. white wine
3. fly a kite
4. nice try
5. nine lives
6. bright light
7. fly high
8. sign on the line
9. fine dining
10. ninety-nine

Practice Sentences

1. Why is the price so high for that design?
2. The wildfire started on Friday night.
3. He was tired after hiking for five hours.
4. It's a nine-hour drive to Iowa.
5. We had lime pie and dry white wine.

/aʊ/ AS IN *HOUSE*

*It is better to keep your m**ou**th closed and let people think you are a fool
than to open it and remove all d**ou**bt.*
Mark Twain

Lips: Start not rounded, but as you move toward /ʊ/, lips begin to close and become tense.
Tongue: Moves from relaxed, low to high position for the /ʊ/.

Common Spelling Patterns for /aʊ/

ou	*found, loud, around, thousand*
ow	*now, down, crowd, vowel*

Word Pairs for Practice

CD 1
Track
62

1. about an hour
2. crowded house
3. downtown
4. loud announcement
5. countdown

6. around the mountain
7. brown couch
8. found out
9. down and out
10. pronounce the vowel

Practice Sentences

CD 1
Track
63

1. I doubt that the clown will say something profound.
2. There are flowers all around the house.
3. Is that your spouse in the brown blouse?
4. The clouds behind the mountain will bring showers.
5. The brown cow is near the fountain.

/ɔɪ/ AS IN *BOY*

CD 1
Track
64

*Don't worry about av**oi**ding temptation. As you get older, it will av**oi**d you.*
Winston Churchill

Lips: Move from slightly rounded, oval position to relaxed, slightly parted position.
Tongue: Relaxed, move from mid-high to high position.

Common Spelling Patterns for /ɔɪ/

oi	*avoid, oil, moist, join*
oy	*enjoy, toy, employ, royal*

Word Pairs for Practice

CD 1
Track
65

1. enjoy the toy
2. spoiled boy
3. appointment in Detroit
4. broiled oysters
5. boiling point

6. annoying noise
7. destroy the poison
8. loyal employee
9. moist soil
10. avoid the moisture

Practice Sentences

CD 1
Track
66

1. He destroyed the poison by flushing it down the toilet.
2. Roy had an appointment in Detroit.
3. Joyce is annoyed and a little paranoid.
4. I was disappointed with Joy's choice.
5. Why is Floyd avoiding Roy?

Chapter Two

VOWELS IN DETAIL

This chapter will give you more detailed knowledge of the most problematic vowel sounds for non-native speakers. You will learn to clearly distinguish between certain sounds that may have seemed very similar to you in the past, and you will learn the common spelling exceptions for some vowel sounds within frequently used words. Memorizing these exceptions will significantly improve your accent.

Review of /I/ and /i/ Sounds

*"**Real ri**ches are the **ri**ches possessed **i**nside."*
B. C. Forbes

The /I/ sound is easy to identify because it is almost always spelled with the letter *i* as in *big*. The /i/ sound is most commonly spelled with two vowels such as *ee* or *ea*, as in *meet*, or *team*. Remember to relax your tongue and lips for the /I/ sound and to make them tense for the /i/ sound.

 Warning: Dangerous Mistake

Confusing /I/ and /i/ may cause embarrassment or can even be offensive.

Do you mean?	*Or?*
/i/	/I/
sheet	shit
beach	bitch
piece	piss

Practice Dialogues

1. a. **Is it** d**i**ff**i**cult?　　　　　　b. No, **it**'s unbel**ie**vabl**y easy**.
2. a. I f**ee**l **i**ll.　　　　　　　　　　b. Dr**i**nk some gr**ee**n t**ea**.
3. a. Pl**ea**se m**ee**t me for d**i**nner.　b. I w**i**ll b**e** there at s**i**x.
4. a. **Is it** expens**i**ve?　　　　　　　b. No, **it i**sn't. **It**'s r**eally** ch**ea**p.
5. a. I n**ee**d a ref**i**ll of th**e**se p**i**lls.　b. Sp**ea**k w**i**th your phys**i**cian.
6. a. **Is** he st**i**ll r**eally** s**i**ck?　　　　b. No, h**e**'s just f**ee**ling a l**i**ttle w**ea**k.
7. a. Th**is is** compl**e**tely d**i**fferent.　b. But **it is i**nteresting, **i**sn't **it**?

Practice Paragraph

Guilty or Innocent?

Let's b<u>e</u> r<u>e</u>alistic. <u>I</u>t's not that d<u>i</u>fficult to s<u>ee</u> that h<u>e</u>'s g<u>ui</u>lty. H<u>e</u> st<u>ea</u>ls, dr<u>i</u>nks, and ch<u>ea</u>ts. He has ch<u>ea</u>ted h<u>i</u>s v<u>i</u>ct<u>i</u>ms, and h<u>e</u> n<u>ee</u>ds to b<u>e</u> <u>i</u>n pr<u>i</u>son. H<u>e</u> d<u>i</u>d th<u>e</u>se terrible th<u>i</u>ngs, yet h<u>e</u> <u>i</u>nsists that h<u>e</u>'s innocent. Who <u>i</u>s h<u>e</u> k<u>i</u>dding? <u>I</u>n the beginning, many p<u>eo</u>ple d<u>i</u>d bel<u>ie</u>ve that h<u>e</u> was <u>i</u>nnocent. But now w<u>e</u> have the ev<u>i</u>dence that w<u>e</u> n<u>ee</u>d. <u>E</u>ven though h<u>e</u> won't adm<u>i</u>t his g<u>ui</u>lt, I fores<u>ee</u> h<u>i</u>m b<u>ei</u>ng in pr<u>i</u>son for at l<u>ea</u>st fift<u>ee</u>n years. Don't you agr<u>ee</u> w<u>i</u>th m<u>e</u>?

 **Advice from a Successful Student**
"When you leave phone messages for people, there's often the option of listening to your message before you send it. I always listen to the message, and if I think my accent is too strong, I record the message again, sometimes several times, until I am satisfied with the way my speech sounds."
Sonja Sokolova, Russia

Review of /ε/ and /æ/ Sounds

Remember that for the /æ/ sound the jaw is more open, and the tongue is down at the floor of your mouth. For the /ε/ sound, the jaw is just slightly down.

Sentence Pairs for Practice

/ε/	/æ/
1. Don't think about the **pest**.	Don't think about the **past**.
2. He gave me a **letter**.	He gave me a **ladder**.
3. **Send** it carefully.	**Sand** it carefully.
4. The **men** helped me.	The **man** helped me.
5. I need a new **pen**.	I need a new **pan**.
6. Do you need to **beg**?	Do you need a **bag**?

Word Pairs in Sentences

1. This **bed** is **bad**.
2. **Dan** is in the **den**.
3. She **said** that she was **sad**.
4. I **guess** I need **gas**.
5. They **laughed** after he **left**.
6. I **bet** that's a **bat**.

Practice Sentences

1. <u>E</u>very m<u>e</u>mber of my f<u>a</u>mily is l<u>e</u>ft h<u>a</u>nded.
2. My b<u>e</u>st fr<u>ie</u>nd Fr<u>a</u>nk is a successful d<u>e</u>ntist.
3. K<u>e</u>nny's b<u>a</u>d h<u>ea</u>dache l<u>a</u>sted s<u>e</u>veral days.

4. Glen drank ten glasses of fresh lemonade.

5. Everyone was happy that he was elected president.

6. Don't forget to thank Dan for his generous present.

Voicemail Message for Practice

You have reached Ellen Edwards. I am sorry I can't answer right now. I am away from my desk. Please leave a message and I will get back to you as soon as I can.

Practice Paragraph

A Trip to France

Next January I'm planning to visit my friends in France. Last time I went there I was only ten or eleven. I would love to go back again. I am taking a class called "French for Travelers." We are memorizing vocabulary and learning the present and past tenses. I want my French to get better and I am practicing every chance I get. I rented a French film and I felt so bad because I didn't understand a word they said. I guess I will have to make extra effort. I want to learn the language and have a better accent so that people can understand me when I am asking for directions and ordering in restaurants.

Review of /ə/, /ɑ/, /ɔ/, and /ou/ Sounds

These sounds are frequently confused. Non-native speakers sometimes do not clearly distinguish the difference between *cup*, *cop*, *cap*, and *cope*.

/ə/	/ɑ/ /ɔ/	/ou/
Remember, the sound /ə/ as in *fun* or *cup* is a neutral vowel, meaning that everything in your mouth is relaxed and the lips are just very slightly open.	In contrast to the /ə/, the /ɑ/ as in *father* and /ɔ/ as in *saw*, require the mouth to be open. The sounds /ɑ/ and /ɔ/ are very similar, except that for the /ɔ/, the lips are a bit more oval in shape and the tongue is slightly tense. However, in many parts of the United States, the /ɑ/ and /ɔ/ are pronounced the same way. For example, many Americans pronounce *hot* and *tall* with the same vowel sound.	For the /ou/ sound, as in *boat*, the lips are rounded and tense.

Warning: Dangerous Mistake

Confusing /ə/, /ɑ/, /ɔ/, and /ou/ may cause embarrassment or can even be offensive.

Do you mean?	Or?
/ə/	/ɔ/
Doug	dog

Also, mispronouncing words like *coke, focus, fork,* and *folk* can cause you to say an inappropriate or offensive word.

Practice Dialogue

CD 1
Track
77

Coffee Tomorrow

/ou/ /ɔ/
John: Hi Nicole. Can you talk?

/ou/ /ɑ/   /ou/ /ɑ/   /ɑ/ /ə/   /ɔ/   /ɔ/   /ɑ/
Nicole: Oh, hi John. Can you hold on? I'm on another call. I'm talking to my boss.

/ou/ /ɑ/   /ə/
John: No problem. I'll wait 'til you're done.

/ou/   /ɔ/   /ɑ/   /ou//ɔ/   /ə/ /ou/ /ɑ/
Nicole: Okay, now I can talk. I am sorry it took so long. What's going on?

/ə/   /ə/   /ə/   /ou/   /ə/   /ɔ/   /ɑ/
John: Nothing much. I just wanted to know if we can meet for lunch or coffee tomorrow.

/ə/   /ɑ/ /ɑ/   /ə/   /ɑ/
Nicole: That sounds like fun. I've been working nonstop and I'd love to get out of the office.

The Problematic *O*

CD 1
Track
78

> *Trouble is only opportunity in work clothes.*
> Henry Kaiser

Words spelled with the letter *o* can cause many frustrations for students of the American accent. You have already learned that the pronunciation of a vowel does not necessarily correspond to the spelling of the vowel. This is especially true of the letter *o*. The letters *o* in the words *job, love,* and *only* are all pronounced differently.

This quote from Helen Keller contains fourteen words spelled with the letter *o* and features all three different vowel pronunciations: "When <u>o</u>ne d<u>oo</u>r of happiness cl<u>o</u>ses, an<u>o</u>ther <u>o</u>pens; but <u>o</u>ften we look s<u>o</u> l<u>o</u>ng at the cl<u>o</u>sed d<u>oo</u>r that we d<u>o</u> n<u>o</u>t see the <u>o</u>ne which has <u>o</u>pened for us." The confusion surrounding the letter *o* for non-native speakers is certainly understandable!

The Neutral Sound /ə/

First, let's look at the most problematic sound with an *o* spelling. It's the neutral sound /ə/, as in *love*, *other*, and *Monday*, which non-native speakers frequently mispronounce as *laav*, *ather*, and *Mahn day*. The wrong pronunciation occurs because the /ə/ doesn't exist in some languages and also because learners are used to this sound usually being spelled with the letter *u* as in *up*, *fun*, and *Sunday*. You will improve your American accent if you simply memorize some very common words with the neutral /ə/ sound that are spelled with an *o*, or *ou*, or even *oo*. Start by studying the pronunciation exceptions in the chart below.

CD 1 Track 79

Memorizing the Exceptions

Words spelled with *o* but pronounced as /ə/.

above	done	money	once	somewhere
another	dove	month	one	son
brother	from	mother	other	ton
color	gonna	none	oven	tongue
cover	love	nothing	some	won
come	Monday	of	something	wonderful
does				

Words spelled with *ou* and pronounced as /ə/.

double	couple	Douglas	enough	rough
country	tough	cousin	touch	southern

Words spelled with *oo* and pronounced as /ə/.

blood	flood

Practice Sentences

1. My c**ou**sin is in an**o**ther c**ou**ntry.
2. I l**o**ve s**o**me **o**f those c**o**lors.
3. He makes a t**o**n of m**o**ney every m**o**nth.
4. My **o**ther br**o**ther c**o**mes **o**nce a m**o**nth.
5. N**o**thing was d**o**ne on M**o**nday.
6. N**o**ne **o**f the ab**o**ve are good en**ou**gh.

Word Pairs in Sentences

The word pairs in each of the sentences below are spelled the same except for one consonant being different. Both words are spelled with an *o*, but this vowel is pronounced differently in each word. The second word of each pair contains the /ə/ sound.

other vowel sound	/ə/	
1. bother	brother	Don't b**o**ther your br**o**ther.
2. Rome	come	When will you c**o**me to R**o**me?
3. bone	done	The dog is d**o**ne with the b**o**ne.
4. Tom	from	Where is T**o**m fr**o**m?
5. pouch	touch	Don't t**ou**ch the p**ou**ch.
6. cough	tough	It's t**ou**gh to have a c**ou**gh.
7. goes	does	He g**oe**s there and d**oe**s it.
8. collar	color	What is the c**o**lor of the c**o**llar?
9. over	oven	Come **o**ver to see my new **o**ven.

Sentence Pairs for Practice

/ɑ/	/ə/
1. You have a good **lock**.	You have good **luck**.
2. Where is that **cop**?	Where is that **cup**?
3. I **shot** it.	I **shut** it.
4. He's a big **boss**.	It's a big **bus**.
5. This is **Don**.	This is **done**.

The American /ɔ/ Sound

In American English the /ɔ/ sound as in *caught* and *all* is very similar to the /ɑ/ sound as in *want* or *hot*. In fact, these two sounds, /ɔ/ and /ɑ/, are so similar in many parts of the United States, that some language experts even claim that they are the same sound. So, while going through these lessons, if you are not able to clearly distinguish between these two vowels, don't worry about it; neither can many native speakers of American English.

Warning: Common Mistake

If you studied English outside of the United States, you might have learned British pronunciation. The vowel sound that is most noticeably different between British and American English is the /ɔ/. In British English, this sound is much more rounded, almost like the /oʊ/. The words "coat" and "caught" sound similar in British English but as you have learned, they are very different in American English. Let's practice pronouncing the differences between these two sounds /ɔ/ and /oʊ/.

Sentence Pairs for Practice

/ɔ/	/oʊ/
1. He's a **bald** man.	He's a **bold** man.
2. Where is the **ball**?	Where is the **bowl**?
3. That's a big **hall**.	That's a big **hole**.
4. Don't **pause** now.	Don't **pose** now.
5. I have a big **lawn**.	I have a big **loan**.

Word Pairs in Sentences

1. I **bought** a new **boat**.
2. There is a **ball** in the **bowl**.
3. Did you **call** about the **coal**?
4. You **ought** to eat **oats**.
5. I was **awed** that he **owed** so much.

Practice Sentences

1. We <u>a</u>ll th<u>ou</u>ght that J<u>oe</u> went to R<u>o</u>me.
2. I b<u>ou</u>ght some cl<u>o</u>thes at the m<u>a</u>ll.
3. The <u>au</u>dience appl<u>au</u>ded when the sh<u>ow</u> was <u>o</u>ver.
4. P<u>au</u>l is g<u>o</u>ing h<u>o</u>me in <u>Au</u>gust.
5. We're g<u>o</u>ing for a w<u>a</u>lk even th<u>ou</u>gh it's c<u>o</u>ld.
6. The <u>au</u>thor wr<u>o</u>te his <u>au</u>tobiography.

CD 1
Track
87

Study Tip

Have you ever heard Americans speak your native language? Practice imitating their accent. This will help you get in touch with the American mouth movements and sounds. For example, when Americans speak Spanish, you will notice that they often prolong the Spanish *o* into an /ou/ sound. "Hola amigo" often sounds like: "<u>ou</u>la amig<u>ou</u>." Similarly, "my friends Ricardo and Roberto" sounds like: "my friends Ricard<u>ou</u> and Robert<u>ou</u>." A similar vowel change often occurs when Americans speak French. The vowel /ɛ/ ends up sounding like /eɪ/. "Je vais au marché" can sound like: "Je v<u>eɪɪɪ</u> au march<u>eɪɪɪ</u>." So, when you speak English, prolong these vowels the same way, and you will be on the right track!

Review of /ɛ/, /æ/, /ɑ/, /ɔ/, /ə/, and /oʊ/

CD 2
Track
1

Here is a quote by Mother Theresa which contains all of the vowels we just finished reviewing:

  /oʊ/ /ɑ/   /ɑ/   /ɛ/   /æ/ /æ/   /ə/   /ə/

"I kn<u>ow</u> G<u>o</u>d will n<u>o</u>t give me <u>a</u>nything I c<u>a</u>n't h<u>a</u>ndle. I j<u>u</u>st wish th<u>a</u>t He didn't tr<u>u</u>st

     /oʊ/ /ə/

me with s<u>o</u> m<u>u</u>ch."

CD 2
Track
2

Let's review the vowel sounds that we have been working on so far. Practice saying the short words below that contain the following vowel sounds: /ɛ/, /æ/, /ɑ/, /ɔ/, /ə/, and /oʊ/.

/ɛ/	/æ/	/ɑ,ɔ/	/ə/	/oʊ/
kept	cap	cop	cup	cope
kettle	cat	cot	cut	coat
best	bass	boss	bus	boast
shell	shadow	Shawn	shun	shown
leg	lack	lock	luck	low
net	gnat	not	nut	note
bet	bat	bought	but	boat
lend	land	lawn	London	loan

Review of /ʊ/ and /u/ Sounds

CD 2
Track
3

Remember, /ʊ/ is a relaxed sound, with the lips almost neutral, just very slightly rounded. By contrast /u/ is a tense sound. The lips are rounded and tense.

Practice Dialogues

1. a. Will you start to c**oo**k s**oo**n?
   b. No, I am still t**oo** f**u**ll to think of f**oo**d.

2. a. Who t**oo**k my c**oo**kie?
   b. Don't l**oo**k at me.

3. a. You sh**ou**ld have had some s**ou**p. It's so g**oo**d.
   b. No thanks, I'm really f**u**ll.

4. a. He's f**oo**lish to walk in the w**oo**ds by himself.
   b. Yes. There are a lot of w**o**lves in those w**oo**ds.
   a. I think that w**o**lves howl when the m**oo**n is f**u**ll.
   b. Is that really tr**ue**?

5. a. Do you like my n**ew** b**oo**ts?
   b. Yes, they're c**oo**l.
   a. And take a l**oo**k at my bl**ue** s**ui**t. It's made of w**oo**l.
   b. To tell you the truth, I w**ou**ldn't wear the bl**ue** s**ui**t if I were y**ou**.
   a. Don't you think it l**oo**ks g**oo**d on me?
   b. I think you sh**ou**ld return it.
   a. And I think you sh**ou**ldn't be so r**u**de!

Comparing /u/ and /yu/

Certain words that contain the letter **u** are sometimes pronounced differently in other English accents. For example, some British speakers often add an extra /y/ sound before the /u/. Students who studied British English in their native countries are often surprised to learn that Americans say "Tooz-day" (for *Tuesday*) instead of the British t+youz-day. Similarly, you may have learned to say "t+you+n" (for *tune*) rather than "**toon**" as Americans do.

Words for Practice

Here are some common words spelled with the letter **u** and pronounced as *oo* rather than as *you*.

attitude	gratitude	reduce	stupid	Tuesday
costume	introduce	seduce	student	tumor
due	opportunity	solitude	studio	tune
duty	produce	Stewart	tube	tutor

Practice Sentences

1. It's your d**u**ty to prod**u**ce it by T**ue**sday.
2. Those st**u**dents like iT**u**nes and YouT**u**be.
3. May I introd**u**ce you to my t**u**tor?
4. The prod**u**cer is in the st**u**dio working on a new t**u**ne.
5. I ass**u**me that it's d**ue** on T**ue**sday.
6. That's a st**u**pid attit**u**de, St**ew**art.

Review of the /ər/ Sound

Life is uncertain. Eat dessert first.
Ernestine Ulmer

The words *work*, *turn*, *bird*, and *early* are all spelled with a different vowel, yet the vowel sound is the same. This frequently happens when a vowel is followed by the letter *r*. The sound remains /ər/. Non-native speakers are frequently tempted to pronounce the vowels as they are spelled, and they make the common mistakes of saying "wore+k" instead of "were +k" (for *work*) and "two+rn" instead of *turn*. Sometimes they will even pronounce *bird* as "beer +d."

Words for Practice

Practice saying the following words with the /ər/ sound. Make sure the vowel sound doesn't change even though the spelling does.

	ER	EAR	IR	OR	UR
1.	her	early	circle	work	turn
2.	serve	earth	dirt	worry	curly
3.	verb	earn	first	worse	burn
4.	were	heard	girl	worm	Thursday
5.	nerd	learn	birthday	world	hurt

Sentences for Practice

1. What were the first words that she learned?
2. I will learn the German verbs by Thursday.
3. It's too early to serve dessert.
4. The third version is worse than the first.
5. It's not worth worrying about another birthday.
6. I heard some curse words at work.
7. They weren't certain that the Earth circles the sun.

Vowels Followed by the /r/ Sound

The quality of a vowel sound often changes when an *r* follows it. There is a slight /ə/ sound that is added after certain vowels, making it sound almost as if the word contains an extra syllable. For example, *fire* sounds like "fai /ə/+ɾ."

Words for Practice

Remember to add an extra /ə/ sound before the /r/ sound as you practice reading these words aloud.

/ɪər/	/ɑər/	/aʊər/	/aɪər/	/oʊər/	/ɛər/
fear	far	hour	hire	four	hair
near	star	sour	tired	tore	there
hear	hard	power	expire	more	care
clear	large	flower	Ireland	bored	stairs

Practice Sentences

1. Take the st**air**s in case of f**ire**.
2. The empl**oy**er is h**ir**ing and f**ir**ing.
3. I h**ear** that it exp**ir**ed on the f**our**th.
4. I can't aff**or**d to shop in that st**ore**.
5. I am n**ear** the cash**ier** by the st**air**s.
6. How f**ar** is **Ir**eland from h**ere**?

Chapter Three

CONSONANTS

This chapter will teach you how to form all of the consonant sounds of American English. You can either study this chapter first to get an in-depth understanding of how consonants are formed, or you can just skip to the next chapter ("Problematic Consonants") and begin practicing the most difficult sounds for non-native speakers. Make sure that you also refer to the "Native Language Guide" at the end of the book, which will tell you which specific consonant sounds you need to focus on in this chapter and in the following one.

Forming American Consonants

When you are learning another accent, it is very helpful to know how the instruments of the mouth work together to produce sound. One reason that you have an accent when you are speaking English is that you are likely not moving your tongue and lips in the same way as a native speaker.

A consonant is a sound that is made when the airflow is blocked by either your lips or your tongue. The different places where this block may occur are called "points of articulation." The point of articulation is, therefore, a point of contact of one part of your mouth with another part. For example, when you produce the sound /p/ (which is spelled with the letter p) your lips come together and close shut. So, the points of contact here are your two lips. The sound /b/ (which is spelled with a letter *b*) is also produced by your lips touching, as is the sound /m/.

Sometimes the points of contact, or points of articulation, occur when the tip of your tongue touches directly behind the upper teeth, a part of your mouth called the gum ridge. The sounds that are produced at this point are /t/, /d/, /n/, and /l/. Another point of contact occurs when the back part of your tongue touches the back part of your mouth, near the throat, as in /g/ and /k/. You don't necessarily need to learn the formal names of the different parts of your mouth, but you should develop an awareness of where the points of contact are. Studying the illustration below will help you do this.

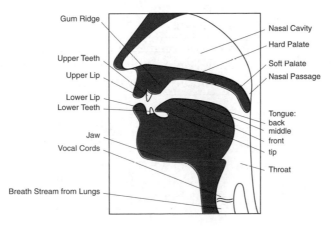

CD 2 Track 13

Voiceless and Voiced Consonants

One way that we categorize consonants is by determining whether they are "voiceless" or "voiced." It's important to know the difference between these types because the length of a vowel that precedes a consonant is determined by whether the consonant that follows it is voiceless or voiced. You will learn more about this later in the chapter. Also, knowing whether a sound is voiceless or voiced will help to correctly pronounce letters such as -*ed* and -*s* at the ends of words. You will learn about this in detail in the next chapter.

First, let's learn how to distinguish between a voiced and a voiceless consonant. Place your fingers in the front, middle part of your neck. Now say /z/ as in the word *zoo*. Now, let's make it longer: *zzzzzzzzzz*. You should feel a vibration in your vocal cords. This is how you know that the /z/ sound is voiced. Now let's try this with the /s/ sound as in the word *sat*. Say /s/. Now let's prolong it: *sssssssss*. This time there was no vibration in your vocal cords, so this consonant is considered unvoiced. That's all there is to it. The tongue and lip positions of the /z/ and /s/ are identical. The only difference between them is vibration or no vibration. Look at the other consonant pairs that are produced exactly the same way, except for the vibration in the vocal cords.

Voiceless and Voiced Consonant Pairs

Voiceless Consonants (vocal cords do not vibrate)		Voiced Consonants (vocal cords vibrate)		How to Produce the Sound
/p/	pet rope	/b/	bet robe	Lips start fully together, then part quickly to produce a small release of air.
/t/	ten seat	/d/	den seed	Tip of the tongue is slightly tense as it firmly touches and then releases the gum ridge.
/k/	class back	/g/	glass bag	Back of tongue presses up against soft palate (back of mouth) and releases.
/f/	fault leaf	/v/	vault leave	Lower lips lightly touch upper teeth; vibration occurs on the lips from the flow of air created.
/θ/	thank breath	/ð/	this breathe	Tip of the tongue touches back of front teeth or edges of front teeth. Air flows out between tongue and teeth.
/s/	sink price	/z/	zinc prize	Sides of tongue touch middle and back upper teeth. Tip of tongue is lowered a bit. Air flows out of middle part of the tongue.
/ʃ/	pressure wish	/ʒ/	pleasure massage	Tip of tongue is down, sides of tongue are against upper teeth on sides of mouth. Air flows out through middle of tongue.
/tʃ/	choke rich	/dʒ/	joke ridge	Tip of tongue is down, sides of tongue are against upper teeth on the side of mouth. Tip of tongue quickly touches gum ridge and then releases.

More Voiced Consonants

Now let's go through the rest of the consonant sounds of English. These consonants are all voiced, but they have no voiceless pair. Make sure that you feel the vibration in your vocal cords as you say them.

/m/	mom from lemon	Lips together. Air flows out of the nose.
/n/	non fun any	Tip of tongue touches gum ridge, and the sides of the tongue touch upper teeth; air any flows out of the nose.
/ŋ/	going spring king	Back of the tongue touches the soft palate; air flows out of the nose.
/l/	love will yellow	Tip of tongue touches upper gum ridge. Tongue is tense. Air comes out on the sides of the tongue, at the corners of the mouth.
/r/	red four card	There are two ways to produce this sound: 1: Tip of tongue curls a bit and then is pulled back slightly. 2: Tip of tongue is down; center of the tongue touches hard palate.
/w/	win lower quiet	Rounded lips as for the vowel /u/ in *moon*. Air flows out through the lips. Tongue is in position for the vowel sound that follows the /w/.
/y/	yes mayor young	Tip of tongue touches lower front teeth. Front of tongue is raised near the hard palate.

The Consonant /h/

This final consonant sound is voiceless and does not have a "voiced pair" that it corresponds to.

/h/	happy behave who	Vocal cords are tense and restricted, back of tongue is pushed against the throat to create friction as the air flows out from the back of the mouth.

Vowel Length and Voiced and Voiceless Consonants

Vowels are **longer** when followed by a **voiced consonant**. They are **shorter** when followed by a **voiceless consonant**. Even short vowels like /i/, /ɛ/, /ə/, and /ʊ/ are prolonged when followed by a voiced consonant.

⚠ Warning: Common Mistake

When you lengthen a vowel, make sure that
you do not change the sound of the vowel.
For example, when you say *hid* make sure that it
doesn't sound like *heed*.

CD 2
Track
15 ## Word Pairs for Practice

	voiceless	voiced		voiceless	voiced
	/s/	/z/		/t/	/d/
1.	advice	advise	4.	mate	made
2.	ice	eyes	5.	hat	had
3.	niece	knees	6.	bet	bed
	/f/	/v/		/k/	/g/
7.	half	have	10.	back	bag
8.	life	live	11.	dock	dog
9.	belief	believe	12.	duck	Doug

CD 2
Track
16 ## Practice Sentences

voiceless	voiced
1. My wallet is in the **back**.	My wallet is in the **bag**.
2. I saw five **bucks** on the floor.	I saw five **bugs** on the floor.
3. He has blue **ice**.	He has blue **eyes**.
4. I heard about the **lice**.	I heard about the **lies**.

CD 2
Track
17 ## Word Pairs in Sentences

1. He told me **lies** about the **lice**.
2. His **eyes** are **ice** cold.
3. There was a **buzz** in the **bus**.
4. The **dog** is on the **dock**.

Stops and Continuants

There is another important way that consonants are categorized, besides whether they are voiced or voiceless. Consonants can either be "stops" or "continuants," depending on whether the airflow is stopped or if it is continued. For example, when we say the /s/ sound we can prolong it by saying "yessssssss." The /s/ sound is considered a continuant because the air flow can continue as long as we have air in our lungs. But if we say a word like "job," we cannot continue the final consonant, /b/. We stop the airflow by closing our lips. Therefore, /b/ is a stop. If we quickly open our lips, we can then "release" the stop and say *job*.

Holding Final Stops

Americans generally do not release many of the final stops. For example, when they say the sound /p/ in the word *stop*, the lips stay closed. No air comes out. This creates almost a silent version of the sound /p/, or a half *p*. We know the *p* is there, but we don't hear all of it. If the lips were released, there would be a slight puff of air.

Let's try another stop: the sound /g/. When you say the word *big*, don't release the /g/. Make sure that your tongue remains up in the back of your mouth when you are done saying the word.

Words for Practice

Pay special attention to the final consonants as you pronounce the words in each column.

	final *p*	final *b*	final *d*	final *t*
1.	stop	club	married	that
2.	cup	job	played	sat
3.	up	sub	sad	it
4.	shop	tub	dad	cut

Final Stops Followed by Consonants

The final stop is always held when the next word within the same sentence begins with a consonant. However, when a word with the final stop is at the end of a sentence, the rule is much more flexible. The final sound can either be held or released.

Word Pairs for Practice

Make sure you hold the final consonant of the first word of the pair.

1. hel**p** him
2. kee**p** talking
3. di**d** that
4. coul**d** go
5. sto**p** that
6. jo**b** market
7. bi**g** park
8. cu**p** cake

Chapter Four

PROBLEMATIC CONSONANTS

This chapter will help you fix the most common consonant errors that non-native speakers of English make. In some cases, the pronunciation of these sounds is exclusive to American English; in other cases, correct pronunciation can be difficult for a non-native speaker if that particular sound does not exist in his or her native language.

The Various *t* Sounds of American English

A happy person is not a person in a certain set of circumstances,
but rather a person with a certain set of attitudes.
Hugh Downs

We'll start with one of the most distinctly American consonants, the letter *t*. The *t* can be pronounced in several different ways, depending on its position in a word and depending on the other sounds that surround it. Sometimes *t* sounds more like a *d* (as in *water* and *atom*), and sometimes it is not pronounced at all (as in *often* and *interview*). Other times it's barely pronounced as in *but* and *cat*. Also, it can change to a different sound when it is followed by an *r* sound, as in *try* or *truth*.

The Held *t*
As a simple awareness exercise, let's first practice saying the /t/ sound so that you get a feeling of where in the mouth it occurs. Repeat saying the *t*: "ttttt." You will notice that the tip of your tongue is touching and releasing your gum ridge, which is the upper part of your mouth, right behind your front teeth. Try it again: "ttttt." This is what we call a fully pronounced *t*. The tongue touches and releases.

Now say the following two words which end with a *t*: cat, right.

Say them again; this time do not release the *t*. Just let your tongue stay on top, touching the gum ridge, with no air coming out when you say the *t*. This is called the "held *t*." The other way to make this kind of silent *t* is just to press the vocal cords together to stop the airflow, and then release.

The letter *t* is generally held at the end of words and before consonants within words. This "held *t*" is very common in American English. Using it will help you to sound more like a native speaker since non-native speakers almost always tend to release the *t* when speaking English. *Note:* You *will* sometimes hear Americans release the final *t*. If they do, it's usually at the end of a phrase or a sentence, or for special emphasis of a word. For example: "That's great!" "It's so hot!" There is no absolute rule about always holding the *t*, but keep in mind that if you release the *t* at the end of *every* word, it *will* sound like a foreign accent.

Words for Practice

1. cut
2. Robert
3. state

4. out
5. present
6. budget

7. list
8. absent
9. met

Word Contrasts for Practice

For the second word of each pair, the final "held t" interrupts and shortens the preceding consonant.

no *t*	*t*		no *t*	*t*
1. can	can't		4. men	meant
2. fall	fault		5. fell	felt
3. star	start		6. car	cart

Did you say *can* or *can't*?

The silent *t* is one of the reasons why you may have a hard time hearing the difference between the words "can" and "can't." Listen for the held "t" for "can't." Also the vowel in the word "can't" is usually longer because negative auxiliaries are stressed more than affirmative auxiliaries within sentences. You can learn more about word stress in Chapter Six.

Held *t* + Consonant

A. Always hold the final *t* when the next word begins with a consonant.

1. it was
2. might do

3. can't go
4. at work

5. didn't like
6. won't need

7. eight weeks
8. budget cut

B. Always hold the *t* when the next letter within the same word is a consonant.

1. football
2. outside

3. lately
4. nightmare

5. atmosphere
6. atlas

7. Atlanta
8. butler

Practice Sentences

1. I migh**t** no**t** do tha**t**.
2. It's no**t** tha**t** grea**t**.
3. He buil**t** tha**t** websi**t**e las**t** nigh**t**.
4. I**t** fel**t** qui**t**e ho**t** in Vermon**t**.
5. Wha**t**?! Tha**t** can'**t** be righ**t**!
6. Ma**tt** wen**t** ou**t** for a bi**t**e to ea**t**.
7. Tha**t** apar**t**ment fel**t** qui**t**e hot.
8. If you ea**t** ou**t** every nigh**t** you'll ge**t** fa**t**.

Study Tip

Make a list of the most common words that are used in your work-place, or if you are a student, the terminology in your field of study. Find out the correct pronunciation of these words. Also, master the pronunciation of the name of the company that you work for and the names of your American co-workers. This will greatly add to your confidence level when you are speaking in professional situations.

Held *t* Before /n/ Sound

When *t* is followed by an /n/ sound within a word, make sure you hold the *t*. For example, when pronouncing *button*, hold the *t* as in *but*, and then add an /n/ without releasing the tongue from the gum ridge: "bu**t** + n."

Words for Practice

1. certain	3. mountain	5. cotton	7. eaten	9. forgotten
2. gotten	4. lighten	6. Britain	8. written	10. frighten

Practice Sentences

1. I will shor**ten** the cur**tain**.
2. He has ea**ten** the ro**tten** food.
3. I'm cer**tain** that it was wri**tten** in Bri**tain**.
4. I've already forgo**tten** the sen**ten**ce.
5. That co**tton** blouse has bu**tton**s.
6. Mar**tin** Luther King and Bill Clin**ton** are famous Americans.

Silent *t* After *n*

The *t* after an *n* is often silent in American pronunciation. Instead of saying *internet* Americans will frequently say "innernet." This is fairly standard speech and is not considered overly casual or sloppy speech.

Words for Practice

CD 2 Track 32

1. interview
2. twenty
3. disappointing
4. accountable

5. dentist
6. intellectual
7. quantity
8. advantages

9. international
10. center
11. cantaloupe
12. plenty

13. Santa Monica
14. Atlanta
15. Orange County
16. Sacramento

Practice Dialogue for Silent t

CD 2 Track 33

a. There are many advantages to working for that international company.

b. I'll be disappointed if they don't call me for an interview.

a. I hear they're looking for someone with interpersonal skills and plenty of energy.

b. It's only twenty minutes from Santa Monica.

When *t* is Between Two Vowels

CD 2 Track 34

When a *t* is between two vowels, it is generally pronounced like a fast /d/ sound. It also sounds the same as the "rolling *r*" sound of many languages, when the tip of the tongue touches the upper gum ridge. This sound is also sometimes called a "tapped *t*" because you quickly tap the tip of the tongue on the gum ridge when pronouncing it.

A *t* becomes a "fast /d/" in the following cases:

A. Between two vowels:	*We don't say:* better	*We say:* bedder
B. Before an "l":	*We don't say:* little	*We say:* liddle
C. After an "r" and a vowel:	*We don't say:* party forty	*We say:* pardy fordy

Note: A *t* does not change to a "fast /d/" sound if it's within a stressed syllable. We don't say: "adack," we say "attack."

Words for Practice

CD 2 Track 35

1. city
2. duty

3. better
4. ability

5. total
6. matter

7. meeting
8. quality

When *t* is Between Two Words

CD 2 Track 36

This "fast /d/" sound also occurs between two separate words when the first word ends with a vowel + *t* and the next word begins with a vowel. Again, this is not sloppy or casual speech; it is a standard American accent.

Word Groups for Practice

1. it is
2. get up
3. try it on
4. eat out
5. at eleven
6. wait a minute
7. what if
8. put it off

Practice Sentences

1. I'll eat it a little later.

2. I bought an auto battery for forty dollars.

3. Peter wrote a better letter.

4. I'd better go to the meeting at eleven.

5. He met her at a computer store in Seattle.

6. It's a pity that he's getting fatter and fatter.

7. Tell the waiter to bring it a little later.

8. He bought a lot of bottles of water.

9. Betty's knitting a little sweater for her daughter.

10. It'll be better if you heat it before you eat it.

The "Fast *d*" Sound

In addition to the standard /d/ sound as in words like *dog*, *day*, and *bed*, there is another kind of /d/ sound that occurs between two vowels and also before an *l*. It sounds exactly like the *t* between two vowels and is often called "fast /d/." Again, it's a sound made with the tip of the tongue quickly tapping the gum ridge.

Word Pairs for Practice

The following word pairs sound the same even though the first word is spelled with a "t" and the second word is spelled with a "d." Since the *d* and *t* are both positioned between two vowels, they sound identical.

1. **medal** — He won a gold **medal** in the Olympics.
   metal — My car is made out of **metal**.

2. **Adam** — His first name is **Adam**.
   atom — An **atom** is the smallest unit of an element.

3. **hit it** — My hand hurts because I **hit it** hard.
   hid it — You can't find it because I **hid it**.

4. **leader** — The president is the **leader** of the country.
   liter — How much is a **liter** of gasoline?

5. **feudal** — There was a **feudal** system in the Middle Ages.
   futile — My effort was totally **futile**.

Words for Practice

1. already	3. Canada	5. ladder	7. middle
2. addict	4. editor	6. product	8. shadow

Word Pairs for Practice

1. add͜ on   2. made͜ it   3. hid͜ it   4. fed͜ up

Practice Sentences for "Fast *d*"

1. I already added it.
2. Adam will edit the middle part.
3. Those products are made in Canada.
4. She had on a Prada dress.
5. I'm fed up with the crowded elevator.

Note: Remember, if the *d* is within a stressed syllable, even if it is surrounded by vowels, the "fast *d*" rule does not apply.

normal *d*	fast *d*
adopt	addict
adore	audit

The /tʃr/ Sound: *tr*

When a *t* is followed by an *r* sound, the *t* changes and becomes an almost /tʃ/ or "ch" sound. To create this sound correctly, say /tʃ/ as in *chain*, but just make the tip of the tongue a bit more tense when it touches the gum ridge, and focus on creating a stop of air.

Practice Words

1. travel	3. tradition	5. translate	7. traffic	9. turn
2. turkey	4. introduce	6. interest	8. extremely	10. terrific

The /dʒr/ Sound: *dr*

When *d* is followed by an *r*, the /d/ sound changes and becomes an almost /dʒ/ sound.

Practice Words

1. drink	3. drop	5. dream	7. drama	9. syndrome
2. children	4. address	6. cathedral	8. hundred	10. laundry

*Practice Dialogues for **tr** and **dr***

1. a. Why do you <u>tr</u>avel by <u>tr</u>ain?
   b. Because the <u>tr</u>affic is so <u>dr</u>eadful.

2. a. What did San<u>dr</u>a tell the a<u>ttor</u>ney?
   b. She told him the <u>tr</u>uth about the <u>dr</u>ugs.

3. a. Have you <u>tr</u>aveled to <u>Tur</u>key?
   b. Yes, that coun<u>tr</u>y has some in<u>ter</u>esting <u>tr</u>aditions.

4. a. I told him a hun<u>dr</u>ed times not to <u>dr</u>ink and <u>dr</u>ive.
   b. I'm sure he'll <u>tr</u>y to stay out of <u>tr</u>ouble.
   a. To tell you the <u>tr</u>uth, I am <u>dr</u>ained from all this <u>dr</u>ama.

The /dʒ/ Sound: *du* and *d + y*

When a *d* is followed by the vowel *u*, they usually blend to create the sound /dʒ/ which is much like the sound *j* makes in a word like *joke*.

Words for Practice

1. gra<u>du</u>al
2. sche<u>du</u>le
3. gra<u>du</u>ation
4. e<u>du</u>cation
5. proce<u>du</u>re
6. indivi<u>du</u>al

Words for Practice

Similarly, *d* followed by *y* usually produces the /dʒ/ sound.

1. Did you?
2. Would you?
3. Could you?
4. Should you?

The /tʃ/ Sound: *tu* and *t + y*

In many words, when a *t* is followed by a *u*, the resulting blended sound is /tʃ/ which sounds like the *ch* in *church*.

1. ac<u>tu</u>ally
2. si<u>tu</u>ation
3. ri<u>tu</u>al
4. adven<u>tu</u>re
5. vir<u>tu</u>al
6. for<u>tu</u>nate
7. sta<u>tu</u>e
8. na<u>tu</u>re
9. punc<u>tu</u>al
10. pic<u>tu</u>re

Similarly, a final *t* followed by a *y* usually calls for the /tʃ/ sound.

1. Don't you?
2. Won't you?
3. Can't you?
4. Aren't you?

Practice Sentences

1. Di**d** **y**ou go to his gra**du**ation?
2. Woul**d** **y**ou take our pic**tu**re?
3. Why can'**t** **y**ou be punc**tu**al?
4. Don'**t** **y**ou like na**tu**re?
5. Ac**tu**ally, this is a for**tu**nate si**t**uation.
6. You're adven**tu**rous, aren'**t** **y**ou?
7. Why won'**t** **y**ou do it gra**du**ally?
8. Can'**t** **y**ou change your sche**du**le?

Words Ending in -*ed*

The final *ed* forms the past tense of regular verbs (such as *needed* and *worked*) and of some adjectives (such as *interested* and *tired*). The *ed* can cause problems for some non-native speakers because it can be pronounced in three different ways: as /Id/, /d/, or /t/. Here are the three rules you need to know when pronouncing -*ed*.

Rule 1

If the last letter of the word is spelled with a *d* or a *t*, the *ed* is pronounced as /Id/ and as a separate syllable.

needed	admitted	attended	decided
avoided	separated	visited	waited

Rule 2

If the last letter of the word ends in a voiced consonant or a vowel sound, the *e* is silent and *d* is pronounced as /d/. (Reminder: Voiced consonants are /b/, /d/, /g/, /v/, /m/, /n/, / r/, /l/, /z/, /dʒ/, /y/, and /ð/.)

opened	changed	earned	pulled
called	closed	loved	showed

Rule 3

If the last letter of the word ends in a voiceless consonant, the *e* is silent and the *d* is pronounced as /t/. (Reminder: Voiceless consonants are /p/, /t/, / k/, /f/, /s/, /ʃ/, /tʃ/, and /θ/.)

passed	helped	laughed	stopped
washed	watched	worked	liked

Practicing the -ed Sounds

In the spaces provided, write the correct past tense sound of *-ed* in the following verbs. (Is it /Id/, /d/, or /t/?)

1. admitted _____
2. controlled _____
3. developed _____
4. dressed _____
5. ended _____
6. exploded _____
7. finished _____

8. hugged _____
9. liked _____
10. marched _____
11. preferred _____
12. pretended _____
13. pulled _____
14. robbed _____

Linking *ed* Ending and a Vowel

Linking is connecting the final sound of one word to the first sound of the following word. You will need to learn to link words together to create smooth, natural speech. This is discussed in much greater detail in Chapter Eight, "Sound Like a True Native Speaker." It is especially important for you to learn to link words with *ed* endings. The final /t/ and /d/ sounds are much easier to pronounce if they are connected to the vowel that follows it.

example:	*sounds like:*
1. stayed in	stay <u>d</u>in
2. turned on	turn <u>d</u>on
3. developed a	develop <u>t</u>a
4. needed a	nee de <u>d</u>a

Words for Practice

1. worried about
2. looked at
3. talked about

4. interested in
5. worked on
6. liked it

More Linking Practice: -ed + it

Practice linking the final consonant to the word *it*.

/Id/ verbs
1. I needed it.
2. I painted it.
3. I attended it.
4. I admitted it.

/t/ verbs
1. I cooked it.
2. I liked it.
3. I watched it.
4. I stopped it.

/d/ verbs
1. I used it.
2. I cleaned it.
3. I changed it.
4. I loved it.

Practice Dialogues for *-ed* Verbs

1. a. What did you think of the movie?
   b. I lik**ed** it a lot.

2. a. What did you do with the money?
   b. I deposit**ed** it in the bank.

3. a. How did you cook the chicken?
   b. I fri**ed** it in oil.

4. a. Is the heater on?
   b. No, I turn**ed** it off.

5. a. When did you paint the room?
   b. I paint**ed** it last week.

Practice Dialogues

The Job Interview

Listen to the *-ed* endings of the past tense verbs and try to determine which of the three possible sounds you hear: /d/, /t/, or /Id/. In the first part of the job interview, each of the *-ed* verbs is followed by a word that starts with a vowel. Make sure you are linking these two words.

Interviewer: Tell me about some of your experiences as a university student.

Job Seeker: I **studied accounting** and finance.

I **graduated at** the top of my class.

I **maintained a** 4.0 GPA.

I **played on** my college basketball team and **participated in** many extra-curricular activities.

I **volunteered at** the homeless shelter.

I **partied every** weekend.

I **dated a** lot of pretty girls.

I **loved every** minute of it.

Interviewer: Describe some of your personal qualities that would make you qualified for this position.

Job Seeker: I am detail-orient**ed** /Id/, highly motivat**ed** /Id/ and organiz**ed** /d/. I am also

focus**ed** /t/ and determin**ed** /d/, and I work well in a fast-pac**ed** /t/ environment.

I have an advanc**ed** /t/ knowledge of computers. I am also

educat**ed** /Id/ and well travel**ed** /d/.

The *th* Sound

"You must <u>do</u> <u>the</u> <u>th</u>ing you <u>th</u>ink you cannot <u>do</u>."
Eleanor Roosevelt

One of the most difficult consonant sounds for non-native speakers is the *th* or / / sound and the /ð/ sound. Remember that for this sound the tip of your tongue should touch the edges of your front teeth, and the tip of the tongue vibrates a bit while air flows out through your tongue and upper teeth. It's also acceptable to just touch the back of the front teeth as long as the air is flowing through.

There are two *th* sounds in English: the voiced *th* as in *that*, and the voiceless *th* as in *think*.

Practice Words for /θ/ (voiceless *th*)

anything	earth	nothing	Thursday
author	ninth	thank	wealthy
both	health	thing	with

Word Pairs for /θ/ (voiceless *th*)

with nothing	both methods
ninth birthday	third month

> ⚠ **Warning: Common Mistake**
>
> **Voiceless *th* Versus *t***
>
> Some non-native speakers incorrectly pronounce the voiceless *th* as a *t* and the following words end up sounding the same.
>
> | /θ/ | /t/ |
> |---|---|
> | thank | tank |
> | bath | bat |

To correct this problem change the position of your tongue by moving it forward to touch the teeth. Also, make sure that there is a flow of air between your tongue and your teeth.

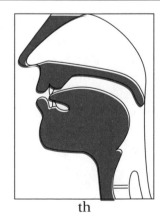

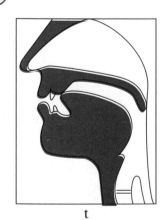

th   t

Practice Words for /ð/ (Voiced *th*)

although	father	this	they
breathe	mother	the	those
clothing	rather	then	weather

Word Pairs for /ð/

that clothing	neither brother
this weather	mother and father

 Warning: Common Mistake

Voiced *th* Versus *d*

Some non-native speakers incorrectly pronounce the voiced *th* as a *d*. The following words end up sounding the same.

/ð/	/d/
they	day
breathe	breed

Again, to correct this problem change the position of your tongue by moving it forward to touch the teeth. Also, make sure that there is a flow of air between your tongue and your teeth.

 Warning: Common Mistake

Make sure that your tongue vibrates under your upper teeth. Do not bite your tongue or press it on your upper teeth too strongly—this will block the flow of air that is required to produce the *th* sound correctly.

Word Contrasts for Practice

Note the difference between the words with *t* and those with the voiceless *th* or /θ/.

	/t/	/θ/		/t/	/θ/
1.	bat	bath	4.	tank	thank
2.	boat	both	5.	team	theme
3.	mat	math	6.	true	threw

Sound Contrasts for Practice

Note the difference between the words with *d* and those with the voiced *th* or /ð/.

/d/	/ð/		/d/	/ð/
1. breeding	breathing	4.	Dan	than
2. dare	their	5.	day	they
3. doze	those	6.	wordy	worthy

Practice Sentences for Voiced and Voiceless *th*

1. Her thirty-third birthday is on the third Thursday of this month.
2. Those three things are worth thousands of dollars.
3. I think that Kenneth is Ethan's father.
4. That new theology doesn't threaten the faithful Catholics.
5. You can buy anything and everything in that clothing store.
6. There are those that always tell the truth.
7. I think that the south has more warmth than the north.
8. I'd rather have this one than that one.
9. Although they're rather thin, they're very healthy.

Practice Sentences for *th* Versus *d*

*It is not because **th**ings are **d**ifficult **th**at we **d**o not **d**are;
it is because we **d**o not **d**are **th**at **th**ings are **d**ifficult.*
Seneca

When the *th* and *d* are very close together, the tip of your tongue must move quickly from touching the teeth to touching the gum ridge so that both sounds can be distinctly heard.

1. **D**on't **d**o **th**at **D**an.
2. What **d**oes **th**at **th**ing **d**o?
3. **D**id **th**ey brea**th**e in **th**e **d**ust?
4. **D**an **th**ought it was **d**ad's bir**thd**ay.
5. How **d**are **th**ey **d**o **th**at!
6. **Th**ey **d**id it **th**e o**th**er **d**ay. **D**idn't **th**ey?

Comparing *th* with *s* and *z*

Some people wrongly pronounce the voiceless *th* as an *s*. They say *sank* and *thank* the same way. They also tend to wrongly pronounce the voiced *th* as a *z*. They say *breeze* and *breathe* the same way. Again, the mistake lies in the position of the tongue. For the *s* and *z*, there is also air passing through the tip of the tongue, but the tongue is *not* touching the teeth. It is touching a little bit behind, on the gum ridge. Pay attention to these tongue positions shown in the illustrations below as you do the following exercises.

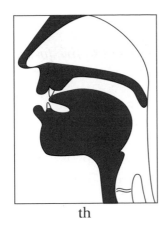

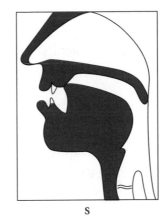

th   s

Word Contrasts for *s* Versus *th*

/s/	/θ/		/s/	/θ/
1. mass	math		3. tense	tenth
2. sank	thank		4. sing	thing

Word Contrasts for *z* Versus *th*

/z/	/ð/		/z/	/ð/
1. close	clothe		3. bays	bathe
2. breeze	breathe		4. Zen	then

Word Pairs for Practice

It's especially difficult to pronounce the *th* sound correctly if the *z* and *s* are nearby. Make sure that all of the consonant sounds are clearly heard. Don't blend them together and don't substitute one for the other.

1. Doe**s th**at
2. What'**s th**at
3. She'**s th**in
4. fi**fth s**tep
5. Wi**th s**ome**th**ing
6. **Sixth s**ong

Practice Sentences for *th* Versus *s* and *z*

1. He'**s** en**th**u**s**ia**s**tic **th**at it'**s** hi**s s**ix**th** bir**th**day.
2. Is **th**at **th**e **z**oo **th**at ha**s th**e **z**ebras?
3. He'**s th**ankful for hi**s** weal**th**.
4. He'**s th**inking about hi**s s**treng**th**s.
5. If it'**s Th**ur**s**day, it'**s th**e **s**ame **th**ing.

The American /r/

Live as if you were to die tomorrow. Learn as if you were to live forever.
Gandhi

Many languages have what is called a "rolling *r*," where the tip of the tongue touches the gum ridge, similar to the /d/ sound, but with a quick and repeated motion. In contrast, the American /r/ is produced in the back of the mouth and the tip of the tongue never touches anywhere inside the mouth. There are different ways to produce the American *r*. Try the two described below and decide which one is easier for you.

Forming the American /r/

Method 1

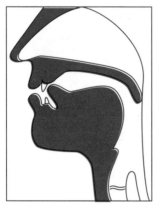

Simply curl the tip of your tongue and pull it back a bit; keep the tongue tense.

Method 2

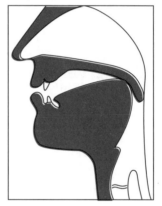

Let the back of the tongue do all the work. Press the sides of your tongue up against the back teeth. In this case, you do not need to curl the tip of the tongue.

Words that End with *r*
Unlike the British *r*, the American *r* is always pronounced. It's never silent. Pay particular attention to *r* when it appears at the end of a word: *for, more, far,* and *teacher*.

Words for Practice

1. more	3. her	5. culture	7. sure
2. here	4. four	6. where	8. car

Word Groups for Practice

All of the following words have an *r* at the end. Make sure you pronounce each one clearly.

1. four door car
2. her younger sister
3. they're never here
4. sooner or later

5. lobster for dinner
6. your older brother
7. four more over there

R Before a Consonant

The *r* before a consonant is always pronounced in American English, but generally not pronounced in British English. Americans say: "morning," "first," "modern." In British English, these words are pronounced as: "moning," "fist," and "moden."

Word Pairs for Practice

1. important information
2. first person
3. hard to understand
4. Northern California
5. early in the morning
6. survive divorce

7. learn German
8. undergoing surgery
9. thirty percent
10. modern furniture
11. March bargain
12. perfect performance

Practice Sentences

1. I spent part of Thursday learning the new computer software.
2. I heard it was a four hour performance.
3. He won a journalism award for his report on Pearl Harbor.
4. Please inform the board about the formal procedure.
5. The terrible storm started yesterday morning.
6. Normally he works in New York.
7. George went to a formal party with his girlfriend.
8. Mark is determined to learn German.
9. I heard that the alternative procedure was better.
10. For your information, they're not divorced.

Story for Practice

Surprise Birthday Party

On Saturday afternoon at four, we're having a surprise birthday party for our daughter Rachel. She'll turn thirteen. Her cousins Charles and Barbara will arrive early to help prepare. We'll take pictures, play cards and some board games. We've ordered a birthday cake and her favorite dessert, strawberry ice cream. We've invited about thirty of her friends and told them to come over before four. We hope all her friends get here by four before Rachel returns from the park. When they're all here, we'll call Mark to bring her over. When they open the front door the lights will be turned off. Her thirty friends will be waiting nervously in the other room. We hope it works out and that Rachel will be really surprised.

Advice from a Successful Student
"I have collected a list of words that are difficult for me to pronounce. I make up sentences from these words and I practice saying them over and over."
Miroslav Nikolic, Serbia

The American /l/

For the American /l/ sound, the tip of the tongue touches the gum ridge behind the upper teeth, just the same as when creating the /t/ and /d/ sounds. See the image below for correct tongue placement. The air stream flows through the sides of the tongue. When the /l/ occurs at the end of a word, make sure you don't release it quickly as you would do with a /t/ or /d/. This will make your /l/ sound foreign. The American /l/ is softer and longer than the /l/ sound of many other languages.

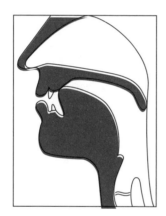

 Warning: Common Mistake

Don't round your lips when you are saying the /l/ sound. This will weaken it and make it sound more like a /w/.

Words for Practice

1. although	4. cold	7. film	10. myself
2. call	5. difficult	8. little	11. people
3. children	6. felt	9. milk	12. will

Word Pairs for Practice

1. tall girl	3. old school	5. cold milk	7. little children
2. felt guilty	4. tall wall	6. gold medal	8. twelve soldiers

l Before a Consonant

For Asian speakers, the /l/ is particularly difficult to pronounce when it is followed by a consonant. If you don't move your tongue correctly, the words *code* and *cold* will sound the same.

Word Contrasts for Practice

Practice the following word pairs, making sure you clearly pronounce the /l/ of the second word.

no /l/	/l/ + consonant	no /l/	/l/ + consonant
1. code	cold	3. toad	told
2. debt	dealt	4. wide	wild

Practice Sentences

1. Jill also doesn't feel well enough to go to school.
2. I'll call Paul and tell him that you'll be late.
3. Twelve people will build a tall wall around the castle.
4. It is doubtful that she'll be able to handle it.
5. He'll bring the cold drink to the ill soldier.
6. The wealthy man sold the building by himself.
7. Don't feel guilty about the spilled milk.
8. The girl told me about the old film.

Long Vowels + /l/

When a long vowel is followed by an *l*, place an extra /ə/sound (schwa) in between. For the word *feel*, say "fee-əl." It's almost as if you are adding an extra syllable.

Words for Practice

	/i/ + əl	/eɪ/ + əl	/aɪ/ + əl	/ɔɪ/ + əl	/u/ + əl
1	feel	sale	mile	oil	tool
2	steal	mail	while	toil	school
3	deal	whale	style	spoil	rule
4	real	pale	smile	foil	fool
5	wheel	fail	file	boil	cool
6	heal	exhale	trial	soil	pool

Word Pairs

1. fail school
2. cool style
3. miles and miles
4. real deal
5. steal the tool
6. file the mail

Understanding /l/ Versus /r/

Keep away from people who try to belittle your ambitions. Small people always do that, but the really great make you feel that you, too, can become great.

Mark Twain

> ⚠️ **Warning: Common Mistake**
>
> If your tongue is not touching the right place, your /l/ will sound like an /r/. For example, the word *wall* might sound like *war*. To correctly pronounce the /l/, make sure that the tip of your tongue is in the front, near the upper front teeth when it touches the top of your mouth. If the tip of your tongue is pulled farther back in the mouth, it might sound like an /r/ instead. Use a mirror to see the position of your tongue for the /l/ sound.

/l/ and /r/ in the final position

Pay attention to the position of your tongue as you practice these two final sounds. Prolong the sounds as you concentrate on what your tongue is doing.

Sound Contrasts for Practice

	final /l/	final /r/		final /l/	final /r/
1.	feel	fear	5.	bowl	bore
2.	deal	dear	6.	tile	tire
3.	stole	store	7.	while	wire
4.	mole	more	8.	file	fire

Consonants + *r* and *l*

When the /r/ or /l/ sound comes after a consonant, make sure that it is strong enough to be clearly heard. Fully pronounce the first consonant before you begin the /r/ or the /l/. Otherwise, the words *fright* and *flight* will end up sounding like *"fight."* You can even add a short /ə/ sound between the two consonants.

Word Contrasts for Practice

	no /r/ or /l/	/r/	/l/
1.	fame	frame	flame
2.	bead	breed	bleed
3.	gas	grass	glass
4.	fee	free	flee
5.	fight	fright	flight
6.	pay	pray	play

Practice Sentences

1. It's always pleasurable to travel first class.
2. He was clearly surprised about the promotion.
3. The president flies in his private airplane.
4. The training program will take place early in the spring.
5. I plan to regularly practice playing the flute.
6. Everyone went to Brenda's surprise party.
7. I traveled to Britain last spring.
8. I frequently fly to Florida to visit my friend.
9. Clara looked truly lovely in her blue blouse.
10. Brian is fluent in French.

Review of /r/ and /l/

Practice Dialogues

1. a. Laura has curly brown hair.
   b. However, her brother Carl has straight blond hair.

2. a. What is that lawyer's overall priority?
   b. Probably to win every trial.

3. a. I am gradually learning to pronounce all the vocabulary correctly.
   b. Really? It's truly wonderful to hear that!

4. a. I heard he speaks several languages fluently.
   b. Yes, he speaks French, English, and Italian fluently.

5. a. Have you heard the fairy tale about Cinderella?
   b. Yes, she was a poor girl who rarely felt pretty.

6. a. Central Park is a great place for rollerblading.
   b. And it's only several minutes from her large apartment.

7. a. He's an incredibly talented flute player.
   b. He also regularly plays the clarinet.

Poems for Practice

Alchemy

I lift my heart as spring lifts up
A yellow daisy to the rain;
My heart will be a lovely cup
Altho' it holds but pain.

For I shall learn from flower and leaf
That color every drop they hold,
To change the lifeless wine of grief
To living gold.
Sara Teasdale

Barter

Life has loveliness to sell,
All beautiful and splendid things,
Blue waves whitened on a cliff,
Soaring fire that sways and sings,
And children's faces looking up,
Holding wonder like a cup.

Life has loveliness to sell,
Music like a curve of gold,
Scent of pine trees in the rain,
Eyes that love you, arms that hold,
And for your spirits still delight,
Holy thoughts that star the night.

Spend all you have for loveliness,
Buy it and never count the cost;
For one white singing hour of peace
Count many a year of strife well lost,
And for a breath of ecstasy
Give all you have been, or could be.
Sara Teasdale

Advice from a Successful Student
"My friend and I are both Chinese and both are studying accent reduction. We get together and speak only in English and we try to correct each others' mistakes. We are able to point out a lot of mistakes to each other even though we are not American. We have learned what our main weaknesses are, and it's now just a matter of reminding each other and practicing in order to break those old habits."

Fang Lee and Mei Wu, China

The /v/ Sound

To produce the /v/ sound correctly, make sure the lower lip touches the upper teeth. (See illustration below.) People who speak quickly have a tendency to drop this sound at the end of words. Others may confuse it with an /f/ sound, and some others change it to a /b/ or a /w/ sound.

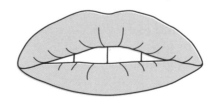

Words for Practice

1. very	4. eleven	7. have
2. verb	5. involve	8. twelve
3. vote	6. achieve	9. five

Practice Sentences

1. Five of David's relatives live in Vienna.
2. Steve and Vivian will come over at eleven.
3. I believe he will move to Vermont in November.
4. Whoever is involved will be investigated.
5. Twelve of us drove to the river near Vegas.
6. Avoid drinking vodka every day.
7. They served flavorful veal and a variety of vegetables.
8. I've been given a favorable evaluation.
9. I would've invited you over but I had a fever.
10. They've never believed my viewpoint.

Understanding /b/ Versus /v/

I've been rich and I've been poor—and believe me, rich is better.
Sophie Tucker

Non-native speakers of some languages have a hard time distinguishing between the /b/ and /v/. Remember, for /v/, the upper teeth touch the lower lip. For /b/, both lips touch and fully close so that no air escapes. Examine the illustrations below to see the difference.

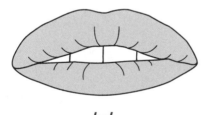

/v/

/b/

Word Contrasts for Practice

	/v/	/b/		/v/	/b/
1.	vest	best	4.	vet	bet
2.	very	berry	5.	curve	curb
3.	vow	bow	6.	vote	boat

Word Pairs in Sentences

1. That's a **very** good **berry**.
2. That's the **best vest**.
3. Can you **vote** on a **boat**?
4. Park next to the **curb** on the **curve**.
5. I **bet** he's a **vet**.

Practice Sentences

1. <u>B</u>everly is <u>v</u>ery <u>b</u>usy de<u>v</u>eloping her new <u>b</u>usiness.
2. <u>V</u>ince lo<u>v</u>es <u>b</u>asket<u>b</u>all and <u>b</u>aseball.
3. <u>B</u>en dro<u>v</u>e to Las <u>V</u>egas in his <u>b</u>lack <u>V</u>ol<u>v</u>o.
4. I <u>b</u>elie<u>v</u>e they'<u>v</u>e <u>b</u>een to <u>V</u>irginia <u>b</u>efore.
5. Did <u>V</u>i<u>v</u>ian ha<u>v</u>e a <u>b</u>irthday in No<u>v</u>em<u>b</u>er?
6. They'<u>v</u>e ne<u>v</u>er <u>b</u>een a<u>b</u>le to pro<u>v</u>e it, ha<u>v</u>e they?
7. Cucum<u>b</u>er and <u>b</u>roccoli are <u>B</u>en's fa<u>v</u>orite <u>v</u>egeta<u>b</u>les.
8. Ga<u>b</u>riel was o<u>v</u>erwhelmed when he won the No<u>b</u>el Prize for the no<u>v</u>el.

The /w/ Sound

*The **qu**estion is not **wh**ether **w**e **w**ill die, but how **w**e **w**ill live.*
Joan Borysenko

The /w/ sound requires the lips to be fully rounded and pushed forward a bit as in the illustration below. Many non-native speakers confuse the /v/ and the /w/ sounds. To avoid this mistake, make sure your bottom lip is not touching your upper teeth when you are saying the /w/. Let's first practice the /w/ to make sure you are pronouncing it correctly. Then we will practice /v/ and /w/ together.

Words for Practice

1. always	3. flower	5. well	7. wife
2. wish	4. work	6. window	8. swim

The /kw/ Sound

CD 3 Track 13

Words that are spelled with *qu* are pronounced as /kw/.

1. quick
2. question
3. require
4. quiet
5. quality
6. frequent

Word Pairs for Practice

CD 3 Track 14

1. white wine
2. always working
3. quick wedding
4. powerful wind
5. weak witness
6. wonderful weekend
7. anywhere you wish
8. twenty flowers
9. windshield wiper
10. frequent question

Practice Dialogue

Winter Weather

a. I wonder when the weather will get warmer.

b. Why are you always whining about the weather?

a. It's always so wet and windy. I would love to go for a quick swim or a walk in the woods.

b. Well, wait a few weeks and it won't be so wet and windy.

a. I wish you were right, but in a few weeks it will still be winter.

b. OK then, we'll have to move west. Maybe to Hollywood, where the weather is warmer.

a. Wow, what a wonderful idea. But wait! Where will we work?

b. We won't have to worry about work once we get there. Hollywood will welcome us. We'll become wealthy movie stars.

a. Wake up and stop your wishful thinking.

Song Lyrics for Practice

"After You Get What You Want You Don't Want It"

After you get what you want, you don't want it
If I gave you the moon, you'd grow tired of it soon

You're like a baby
You want what you want when you want it
But after you are presented
With what you want, you're discontented

You're always wishing and wanting for something
When you get what you want
You don't want what you get

And tho' I sit upon your knee
You'll grow tired of me
'Cause after you get what you want
You don't want what you wanted at all

Excerpt from a song by Irving Berlin

Understanding /v/ Versus /w/

You are never given a wish without also being given the power to make it come true.
You may have to work for it, however. "
Riard Bach

Note the different lip positions in the illustrations below as you work through the following exercises. Do not confuse /w/ with /v/!

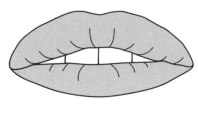

/v/

/w/

Word Contrasts for Practice

	/v/	/w/		/v/	/w/
1.	vine	wine	4.	vest	west
2.	vow	wow	5.	verse	worse
3.	vet	wet	6.	veal	wheel

Word Pairs for Practice

1. every week
2. very well
3. wise investment
4. weigh the vegetables
5. west Virginia
6. wonderful voice
7. white van
8. valuable watch
9. wear the vest
10. weird video

Practice Sentences

1. Victor's wife Vicky was very wise.
2. It was very warm all week.
3. Don't wear your valuable watch this weekend.
4. When will Vick weigh the vegetables?
5. Were you involved in Vivian's wedding plans?
6. Will we view the video on Wednesday?

The /s/ and /z/ Sounds

/z/ /s/   /z/   /z/   /s/   /s/ /z/   /z/   /z/ /s/

A bird doe<u>s</u>n't <u>s</u>ing becau<u>s</u>e it ha<u>s</u> an an<u>s</u>wer, it <u>s</u>ings becau<u>s</u>e it ha<u>s</u> a <u>s</u>ong

Maya Angelou

The letter *s* is sometimes pronounced as a /z/ sound and sometimes as a /s/ sound. When *s* follows a consonant, there are rules for pronunciation, but when it follows a vowel there are no rules—so it's best to just memorize the exceptions. Studying the four basic rules below will also be helpful to you.

 Warning: Common Mistake

The letter *z* is never pronounced as an /s/ sound. If your native language is Spanish, compare the way Americans pronounce common Spanish last names (such as "Gomez" or "Alvarez") with the way you pronounce them in Spanish.

Rule 1

When an *s* follows a *voiceless* consonant, it is pronounced as /s/.

books	stops	makes	likes
eats	cats	helps	surfs

Rule 2

When an *s* is followed by a *voiced* consonant or a vowel, it is pronounced as /z/.

eggs	beds	lives	cars
comes	boys	loans	feels

Rule 3

Double *s* is pronounced as /s/.

boss	less	success
massive	lesson	essay

exceptions: po<u>ss</u>ession, sci<u>ss</u>ors, de<u>ss</u>ert (*ss* sounds like /z/)

Rule 4

An extra syllable is added to words that end with certain consonant sounds followed by *s*. These include:

sound:	consonant:	examples:
/dʒ/	*g*	*manages, changes*
/ʃ/	*sh*	*washes, dishes*
/tʃ/	*ch*	*churches, matches*
/s/	*s, ss, c*	*bosses, faces*
/ks/	*x*	*boxes, faxes*

Study Tip

Memorize these very common words that have a final *s*.
The *s* is pronounced as /z/ and *not* as /s/.

was	his	these	goes	because
is	hers	those	does	
as	has	whose	always	

⚠ Warning: Common Mistake

Note that the *s* in the prefix *dis–* is pronounced as
/s/ and not as /z/.

disagree	disobey	disappear
disorder	disapprove	disability

Verbs and Nouns and the Letter *s*

The following words spelled with an *s* have a /z/ sound when they are verbs but have a /s/
sound when they are nouns.

noun:	verb:		noun:	verb:
/s/	/z/		/s/	/z/
1. use	to use		4. house	to house
2. abuse	to abuse		5. excuse	to excuse
3. close	to close		6. advice	to advise

Dialogues for Practice

a. Do you still **use** /z/ this?

b. No, I have no **use** /s/ for it any more.

a. Where will they **house** /z/ their guests?

b. They have a guest **house** /s/.

a. Does he **abuse** /z/ drugs?

b. Yes, he's getting help for his drug **abuse** /s/.

/z/
a. Please **excuse** me.
/s/
b. I don't accept your **excuse**.

/z/
a. Would you **close** the door?
/s/
b. You do it. You're **close** to it.

/z/
a. Can you **advise** me on this?
/s/
b. Sure, I can give you some **advice**.

Practice Sentences

Remember to pronounce all of the final /s/ sounds of plural nouns. Also pronounce the final /s/ of verbs in the third person singular form (*he*, *she*, *it*). Say the following sentences quickly, making sure that you are not forgetting the *s* endings.

1. A dishwasher wash**es** dish**es**.
2. A bus driver driv**es** bus**es**.
3. A mechanic fix**es** car**s**.
4. A teacher teach**es** student**s**.
5. A watchmaker mak**es** watch**es**.
6. A real estate agent sell**s** hous**es**.

 Warning: Common Mistake

Make sure you are not pronouncing the words *this* and *these* the same way.

	s sound is:	vowel sound is:
this	/s/	/I/ (as in *sit*)
these	/z/	/i/ (as in *meet*)

examples:
I like **this** book. I like **these** books.

Story for Practice
Mark's Day

Every morning he ge/s/ts up early, brush/iz/es his teeth, wash/iz/es his face, and ea/s/ts breakfast.

He kiss/iz/es his wife and kid/z/s goodbye. He take/s/s two bus/iz/es to work. He usually mana/iz/ges

to get to work before his coworker/z/s. He read/z/s his email, check/s/s messa/iz/ges and return/z/s

phone call/z/s. He speak/s/s with his colleague/z/s and client/s/s and conduct/s/s meeting/z/s.

He focus/iz/es on his daily tas/s/ks and like/s/s to take only 30 minute/s/s for lunch.

The /ŋ/ Sound: Pronouncing *ng*

*There's as much risk in doi**ng** nothi**ng** as in doi**ng** somethi**ng**.*
Trammell Crow

In American English, the final *g* in the word ending *-ing* should not be dropped, but it should not be over pronounced either.

Don't say: *"I'm goin shoppin."* And don't say *"I'm going shopping"* by releasing the *g* too strongly. To create the /ŋ/ sound raise the back of the tongue and let it touch the soft palate, which is the soft area at the rear of your mouth. Don't release your tongue when you pronounce /g/, or just release it slightly. The mistake of saying "goin' shoppin' " is that the tip of the tongue is touching the area right behind the upper front teeth to create a /n/ sound. And if you say *"going shopping,"* the mistake is that the /g/ is released too much.

Words for Practice
1. doing	4. listening
2. teaching	5. being
3. coming	6. going

Word Pairs for Practice
1. doing nothing	4. wedding ring
2. something wrong	5. bring everything
3. looking young	6. feeling strong

Practice Sentences
1. Don't bring the wrong rings to the wedding.
2. I love running, skiing, and swimming.
3. He's looking young and feeling strong.
4. They sell anything and everything in that clothing store.

Confusing *n* and *ng* Endings

Remember, for /n/ as in *thin*, the tip of the tongue touches the gum ridge, just behind the teeth. For the /ŋ/ sound as in *thing* the tip of the tongue is down, not touching anywhere. The back of the tongue is up, touching the soft palate which is located in the back of your mouth. Examine the illustrations below to see the difference.

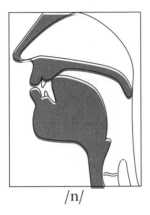

/n/

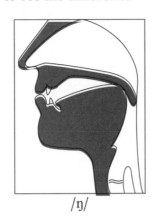

/ŋ/

Word Contrasts for Practice

/n/	/ŋ/		/n/	/ŋ/
1. thin	thing	4.	win	wing
2. ran	rang	5.	ban	bang
3. fan	fang	6.	run	rung

Consonant Clusters

> *Ho**ld** yourse**lf** re**sp**onsi**bl**e for a higher standa**rd** than anybody e**xp**e**ct**s of you.*
> *Never e**xc**use yourse**lf**.*
> Henry Ward Beecher

Two or more consonant sounds together are called "consonant clusters." Many languages do not have any words with consonant clusters. Therefore, when native speakers of these languages speak English, they tend to skip one or more of the consonants. Make sure you pronounce every consonant sound! Pay special attention to words spelled with the letter *x* since it represents a blend of two consonant sounds: /ks/ or /gz/. Also, many verbs that take *-ed* in the past tense consist of consonant clusters; for example: *wa**tched**, sto**pped**, pi**cked***.

Common Words with Consonant Clusters

say:	*don't say:*
insta**ntl**y	instan...ly
ho**pef**ully	ho...fully
apa**rt**ment	apar...ment
wo**rked** (sounds like "wo**rkt**")	wor...
te**xtb**ook (sounds like "te**kst**book")	tes...book
e**xtr**a (sounds like "e**kstr**a")	estra
vo**dk**a	vo...ka
stre**ngth**	stren...th
reco**gn**ize	reco...nize

Different Sounds for *x*

If the vowel following an *x* is stressed, the *x* is pronounced as /gz/, as in *examine* and *exist*. If an *x* is followed by a consonant, or if it's at the end of a word, it is pronounced as /ks/, as in *expert* and *tax*. Also, note that a double *c* often produces an *x* or /ks/ sound, as in the word *accent*. If these two sounds don't occur together in your native language, be very careful to pronounce both of these consonant sounds.

Words for Practice for *x* and *cc*

1. extreme	4. extra	7. extract	10. exact
2. accept	5. success	8. context	11. expect
3. next	6. accident	9. extinguish	12. example

Word Contrasts for Practice

Make sure you pronounce the words in the following pairs differently. Notice that the first word contains just an *s* sound; the second word contains a *k* and an *s* sound and is spelled with the letter *x*.

/s/	/ks/		/s/	/ks/
1. nest	next		4. aspect	expect
2. test	text		5. contest	context
3. session	section		6. mass	Max

Practice Dialogue

a. How did you do on the en**tr**ance e**x**am?
b. I wasn't so su**cc**essful. I e**xp**ected to pass, but it was e**xtr**a difficul**t**.
a. Did you study all the se**cti**ons of the te**xt**book?
b. Yes, but I have to study harder on the ne**xt** te**st** and ho**pef**ully I will be su**cc**essful.
a. When do you e**xp**ect to take the ne**xt** te**st**?
b. I will atte**mpt** it in Se**pt**ember. I'll be e**cst**atic if I get a**cc**e**pt**ed at the be**st** school.

Words Ending with *ts*

Make sure you pronounce both the /t/ and the /s/ sounds in the following words. The /t/ will need to be pronounced softly in order to ensure a smooth transition to the /s/.

Words for Practice

1. it's	3. states	5. what's
2. that's	4. lasts	6. doubts

Word Contrasts for Practice

Make sure you pronounce the words in the following pairs differently. The first word contains just an /s/ or /z/ sound, and the second word contains a /t/ and an /s/ sound.

/s/ or /z/	/ts/		/s/ or /z/	/ts/
1. is	its		5. was	what's
2. stays	states		6. pains	paints
3. less	lets		7. knees	needs
4. fax	facts		8. lies	lights

Practice Sentences

1. There are three flights to the United States.
2. She adds and subtracts the costs.
3. Please give the dates to the courts.
4. The applicants signed the contracts.
5. He accepts the facts about the Democrats.

Pronouncing the *ds* Cluster

Make sure you pronounce *both* the /d/ and /z/ sounds in the following words. The /s/ is pronounced like a /z/ sound because it's followed by /d/, which is a voiced consonant. The /d/ will need to be pronounced softly in order to ensure a smooth transition to the /z/.

Words for Practice

1. needs	3. sends	5. kids
2. decades	4. friends	6. sounds

Word Contrasts

Make sure that you that you pronounce the following word pairs differently. The first word contains just a /z/ sound and the second word contains a /d/ and a /z/ sound.

/z/	/dz/		/z/	/dz/
1. fines	finds		4. rise	rides
2. cars	cards		5. lens	lends
3. fees	feeds		6. bills	builds

Practice Sentences

1. David's and Ed's kids are friends.
2. She feeds the cats and cleans the yards.
3. The brides got diamonds from their husbands.
4. He accepts rides from friends.
5. He needs the facts about the debts.

Chapter Five

SYLLABLE STRESS

A syllable is a small unit of speech that consists of a vowel, or a vowel and one or more consonants. Stressed and unstressed syllables form the basis of the rhythmic pattern of English words.

Many languages place the same amount of stress on each syllable. For example, in many languages the word banana is pronounced as:

‾ba ‾na ‾na   (All three syllables are stressed equally.)

In English, we pronounce the word as:

     ‾

‾ba **na** ‾na   (The second syllable is stressed.)

The vowel within the stressed syllable is longer, louder and higher in pitch. The vowel within the unstressed syllable is reduced and becomes a neutral, short vowel called the "schwa" and is pronounced as /ə/. It can be spelled with *a*, *e*, *i*, *o*, or *u*. All of the five vowels can sound the same if they are part of a reduced syllable. As you can see, it is more important to know which syllable is stressed than how the word is spelled. If people don't understand a particular word you are saying, chances are you stressing the wrong syllable.

Note: Phonetically, *banana* looks like this: /bə 'nænə/. The small accent symbol in front of the /n/ indicates that the syllable that follows is stressed. Your dictionary may have different stress markers.

Stressed and Reduced Vowels

Listen to the following word pairs and notice the changes in the vowel sounds, depending on whether the syllable is stressed or reduced. The first word of each pair has only one syllable, so the vowel must be fully pronounced. The second word has two syllables, with the second syllable reduced. Even though the ending of the second word is spelled exactly the same as the first word, the vowel is pronounced differently because it's part of the reduced syllable.

	full vowel	reduced vowel
	one syllable	unstressed second syllable
1.	/æ/ m<u>a</u>n	/ə/ salesm<u>a</u>n
2.	/oʊ/ p<u>o</u>se	/ə/ purp<u>o</u>se
3.	/ɛɪ/ r<u>a</u>ce	/ə/ terr<u>a</u>ce
4.	/ɛɪ/ l<u>a</u>te	/ə/ chocol<u>a</u>te
5.	/ɔ/ c<u>or</u>d	/ə/ rec<u>or</u>d
6.	/ɛɪ/ r<u>a</u>ge	/ə/ cour<u>a</u>ge
7.	/æ/ f<u>a</u>st	/ə/ breakf<u>a</u>st
8.	/æ/ l<u>a</u>nd	/ə/ Engl<u>a</u>nd

Now listen to vowel changes of words that have a reduced *first syllable*.

	full vowel	reduced vowel
	stressed	unstressed first syllable
1.	/ɑ/ c<u>o</u>n	/ə/ c<u>o</u>ntrol
2.	/æ/ <u>a</u>d	/ə/ <u>a</u>dvice
3.	/æ/ l<u>a</u>g	/ə/ l<u>a</u>goon
4.	/ɑ/ p<u>o</u>d	/ə/ p<u>o</u>diatrist
5.	/ɔ/ b<u>a</u>ll	/ə/ b<u>a</u>lloon
6.	/ɛ/ r<u>e</u>d	/ə/ r<u>e</u>duce
7.	/ɔ/ <u>o</u>ff	/ə/ <u>o</u>ffend
8.	/æ/ m<u>a</u>t	/ə/ m<u>a</u>terial
9.	/ɔ/ <u>or</u>	/ə/ <u>or</u>dain
10.	/æ/ m<u>a</u>d	/ə/ M<u>a</u>drid

Dangers of Stressing the Wrong Syllable

Stressing the wrong syllable sometimes creates misunderstandings because people think you are pronouncing a completely different word. The following words are great examples of why syllable stress is such an important component of the American accent.

1. *noble*   honorable, distinguished, aristocratic
   Nobel   a prestigious award of achievement
   "He won the **Nobel** Prize for his **noble** effort."

2. *invalid*   a sick or disabled person
   invalid   not valid, void
   "The **invalid** has an **invalid** permit."

3. *personal*   individual, private
   personnel   a group of people employed in an organization or a place of work
   "Some of the **personnel** have some **personal** problems."

4. *eligible*   worthy of choice, suitable, legally qualified
   illegible   impossible or hard to read
   "You won't be **eligible** for that position if your handwriting is **illegible**."

5. *pronouns*   parts of speech that substitute for nouns are pronouns such as *he* and *she*
   pronounce   to say words, to utter
   "Can you **pronounce** those **pronouns** correctly?"

6. *comedy*   a humorous drama or play
   committee   a group of people elected or appointed to perform a function
   "The **committee** watched a **comedy**."

7. *advantages*   benefits or gain
   advantageous beneficial, useful
   "It would be **advantageous** to learn about the **advantages** of that method."

8. *decade*   ten years
   decayed   become rotten or ruined
   "Their relationship has **decayed** in the past **decade**."

9. *access*   ability or right to enter
   excess   extra, additional
   "Do you have **access** to the **excess** data?"

10. *content* (noun)   the subject matter of a book, speech, etc.
    content (adjective)   satisfied and happy
    "Are you **content** with the **content** of that letter?"

11. *career*   profession
     carrier   a person or company that carries or transports something

"He had a **career** working for an aircraft **carrier**."

12. *discus*   a heavy disc of metal thrown in an athletic competition
     discuss   to talk over in detail, to examine in speech or writing

"The **discus** throwers **discussed** the competition."

Study Tip

Make a list of words commonly used at your workplace or in your field of study. Ask a colleague or classmate who is a native speaker to pronounce the words for you as you record them. Listen to the recording, carefully noting which syllable is stressed.

General Rules for Stress Placement

This section will give you some general guidelines and patterns of American English syllable stress. Keep in mind that there are many exceptions to these rules and that English syllable stress can be quite irregular. Get into the habit of using your dictionary or asking native speakers to pronounce new or confusing words for you.

Two-Syllable Words		
	NOUNS	VERBS
	Stress the first syllable	Stress the second syllable.
1.	action	pro**duce**
2.	paper	ach**ieve**
3.	building	apply
4.	concert	succeed
5.	teacher	attach
6.	father	employ
7.	window	include
8.	garden	destroy

Noun and Verb Pairs

The following pairs of nouns and verbs are spelled the same but pronounced differently because of changing syllable stress. Make sure you reduce the vowel in the unstressed syllable. First you will hear the noun, and then the verb.

NOUNS	VERBS	NOUNS	VERBS
1. **ad**dict	**ad**dict	11. **ob**ject	ob**ject**
2. **con**duct	con**duct**	12. **pres**ent	pre**sent**
3. **con**flict	con**flict**	13. **pro**duce	pro**duce**
4. **con**test	con**test**	14. **prog**ress	pro**gress**
5. **con**vert	con**vert**	15. **reb**el	re**bel**
6. **con**vict	con**vict**	16. **rec**ord	re**cord**
7. **de**fect	de**fect**	17. **re**search	re**search**
8. **de**sert	de**sert**	18. **sub**ject	sub**ject**
9. **in**crease	in**crease**	19. **sus**pect	sus**pect**
10. **in**sult	in**sult**		

Note: Some of the above words have completely different meanings in the verb and noun forms.

Practice Sentences

Underline the stressed syllables in the verbs and nouns in bold letters. To check your answers, listen to the audio.

1. The singer wants to **record** a new **record**.
2. The drug **addict** is **addicted** to heroin.
3. He **insulted** me with a rude **insult**.
4. I would like to **present** all of the **present** members.
5. This **permit permits** you to park your car here.
6. They **protested** in the **protest**.
7. Do you **object** to this **object**?
8. The **convict** was **convicted** again.
9. I **suspect** that they caught the **suspect**.
10. They are going to **contest** the results of the **contest**.

Practice Dialogue

Once again, underline the stressed syllables in the bold words before listening to the audio.

a. Have you heard? The police caught the **suspect**!
b. Do you mean the one who is **suspected** of robbing the bank?

a. Yes, I heard that he had a criminal **record**.
b. Oh really? What crime was he **convicted** of?

a. He's a drug **addict** who has been robbing banks to support his **addiction**.
b. How many years do you think he will spend in prison?

a. A maximum of ten years. But he might be released early on good **conduct**.

b. If he **conducts** himself badly and **insults** the prison guards, I wonder if his sentence will be **increased**.

c. I don't know. I haven't heard of a prison term **increase** for **insults** and bad **conduct**.

Words Ending in *-tion* and *-ate*

Verbs that end with *-ate* have a stress on the first syllable. Nouns ending with *-tion* however, have a stress on the syllable before the suffix. Examine the examples in the chart below.

CD 3 Track 35

	Verbs that end in *-ate*	Nouns ending in *-tion*
	Stress is on the first syllable	Stress is on the syllable that precedes the suffix *-tion*
1.	**ac**tivate	acti**va**tion
2.	**cel**ebrate	cele**bra**tion
3.	con**grat**ulate	congratu**la**tion
4.	**dem**onstrate	demon**stra**tion
5.	**do**nate	do**na**tion
6.	**frus**trate	frus**tra**tion
7.	**im**itate	imi**ta**tion
8.	**lo**cate	lo**ca**tion

-ate Endings of Verbs and Nouns

CD 3 Track 36

Note that the *-ate* word ending is pronounced fully in verbs but is reduced in adjectives and nouns. For example, the *-ate* ending of the word *separate* is pronounced /eɪt/ when it is a verb and /ɪt/ when it is a noun.

Word Pairs for Practice

1. a. separate /eɪt/ (verb)   They have decided to **separate**.
   b. separate /ɪt/ (adjective)   They will live in **separate** houses.

2. a. alternate /eɪt/ (verb)   She **alternates** between feeling happy and sad.
   b. alternate /ɪt/ (adjective)   Do you have an **alternate** plan?

3. a. graduate /eɪt/ (verb)   He will **graduate** next spring.
   b. graduate /ɪt/ (noun)   He will be a college **graduate**.

4. a. estimate /eɪt/ (verb)   Can you **estimate** the cost of the repairs?
   b. estimate /ɪt/ (noun)   I would like to have an **estimate** of the costs.

5. a. duplicate /eɪt/ (verb)   I will **duplicate** this document.
   b. duplicate /ɪt/ (noun)   Please make a **duplicate** of it.

6. a. appropriate /eɪt/ (verb)   They city **appropriated** the money for the
                                     new park.

   b. appropriate /ɪt/ (adjective)   It was an **appropriate** decision.

More Stressed Suffixes

Look for words with the following suffixes: *ee, ette, ique, ese, eer,* and *ain.* The suffix is always stressed in these words

1. employ**ee**	4. cass**ette**	7. Japan**ese**	10. volunt**eer**
2. train**ee**	5. un**ique**	8. Chin**ese**	11. main**tain**
3. cigar**ette**	6. bout**ique**	9. engin**eer**	12. exp**lain**

Rules for Prefixes

Sometimes the prefix is stressed and other times it's not. Prefix + verb combinations usually have second syllable stress. Here are a few examples.

over**sleep**	under**stand**	out**live**	re**write**
over**do**	under**take**	out**perform**	re**do**

However, if the prefix + the root word function as a noun, the first syllable is stressed:

oversight	**under**taker	**re**fill	**out**sourcing
overdose	**under**wear	**re**peat	**out**come

With reflexive pronouns, the last syllable is stressed. Note these common examples:

my**self**	him**self**	it**self**
your**self**	her**self**	our**selves**

Practice with Prefixes

Practice saying the following groups of words with the same prefixes, paying attention to the changes in stress. In the nouns, stress the prefix. In the verbs, stress the root word.

PREFIX	Prefix + root word = NOUN	Prefix + root word = VERB
	Stress the prefix	Stress the root word
pre–	**pre**view, **pre**fix	pre**vent**, pre**pare**, pre**dict**, pre**cede**, pre**fer**, pre**tend**
per–	**per**mit	per**form**, per**suade**, per**mit**
pro–	**pro**duct, **pro**cess, **pro**fit, **pro**gress, **pro**ject, **pro**gram	pro**duce**, pro**tect**, pro**pose**, pro**ject**, pro**long**, pro**fess**, pro**mote**
mis–	**mis**chief, **mis**print, **mis**fit	mis**place**, mis**quote**, mis**read**
con–	**con**cert, **con**test, **con**flict, **con**gress, **con**cept, **con**tent,	con**fess**, con**trol**, con**duct**, con**fuse**, con**firm**, con**sent**, con**sole**
com–	**com**plex, **com**pound	com**pete**, com**plain**, com**pare**, com**pose**, com**pute**
ob–	**ob**ject	ob**serve**, ob**tain**, ob**sess**, ob**scure**, ob**struct**
sub–	**sub**ject, **sub**urb, **sub**way	sub**tract**, sub**mit**, sub**scribe**
ex–	**ex**pert, **ex**ile, **ex**cerpt	ex**plain**, ex**tract**, ex**hale**, ex**cuse**, ex**change**, ex**ceed**, ex**clude**, ex**cite**
de–	**de**tail, **de**fect, **de**crease	de**ny**, de**mand**, de**fend**
dis–	**dis**count, **dis**course, **dis**trict	dis**cuss**, dis**trust**, dis**turb**
a–	**a**ccess, **a**ddict, **a**nchor	a**gree**, a**pply**, a**dmit**, a**dore**, a**fford**, a**lert**, a**pplaud**, a**pprove**, a**rrange**, a**ttack**

Practice Paragraph

Underline the stressed syllables in the highlighted verbs and nouns.

The Protest

The **protesters** gathered in front of the government building **expecting** to **confront** the **elected** officials. They were **protesting** the recently **uncovered** corruption. It is **believed** that the officials were inside the building **discussing** the **conflict**. The crowds threatened to **disrupt** the meeting. Some workers **complained** about **receiving** threats from the **protesters**. The mayor **confirmed** that he would **conduct** an investigation and try to **resolve** the **conflict**. The sheriff will **assist** him to **compile** all the **details** of the investigation. The mayor **assured** the **public** that he would make an **effort** to **protect** the citizens from further corruption.

Study Tip

Practice reading aloud, underlining longer words and determining syllable stress by looking in the dictionary. Your dictionary may come with an audio CD which will help you hear the correct word pronunciation.

Syllable Stress Changes

When a word changes from a noun to a verb or to an adjective or adverb, frequently the stress placement changes as well. Listen to these common words that non-native speakers tend to mispronounce (read across).

1. **pol**itics	po**li**tical	poli**ti**cian
2. **phot**ograph	photo**gra**phic	pho**tog**raphy
3. com**pete**	com**pet**itive	compe**ti**tion
4. e**con**omy	eco**nom**ical	e**con**omize
5. **dem**ocrat	de**moc**racy	demo**crat**ic
6. **fam**ily	fa**mil**iar	famili**ar**ity
7. **nec**essary	nece**ssar**ily	ne**cess**ity
8. **hos**pital	hospi**tal**ity	hos**pit**able
9. **orig**in	origi**nal**ity	o**rig**inal
10. me**chan**ic	**mech**anism	me**chan**ical
11. de**fine**	defi**ni**tion	**def**initely
12. **var**y	va**ri**ety	vari**a**tion
13. **cour**age	cou**ra**geous	
14. **prob**ably	proba**bil**ity	
15. ge**og**raphy	geo**gra**phic	
16. **mem**ory	me**mor**ial	
17. **Can**ada	Ca**nad**ian	
18. ig**nore**	**ig**norance	

Sentence Pairs for Practice

Underline the stressed syllables in the highlighted words. To check your answers, listen to the audio.

1. He likes **politics**.
   He wants to be a **politician**.

2. I love **photography**.
   Do you take a lot of **photographs**?

3. He studied **economy**.
   He is an **economical** shopper.

4. Do you know that **family**?
   Yes, they're **familiar** to me.

5. He is a very good **mechanic**.
   He is fixing the **mechanism**.

6. Their opinions **vary**.
   There is a **variety** of opinions in the room.

7. We celebrate **Memorial** Day.
   It's in **memory** of the veterans.

8. Do you know the **origin** of your name?
   No, it's pretty **original**.

9. He is a registered **Democrat**.
   He watched the **democratic** debate on TV.

10. It is not **necessary** to do that.
    I don't **necessarily** agree.

11. He likes to **compete**.
    He's always been very **competitive**.

Practice Paragraph

Underline the stressed syllables in the highlighted words. Check your answers by looking in the dictionary.

American Declaration of Independence

When in the Course of human **events** it **becomes** **necessary** for one people to **dissolve** the **political** bands which have **connected** them with another and to **assume** among the powers of the earth, the **separate** and equal station to which the Laws of **Nature** and of Nature's God **entitle** them, a **decent** **respect** to the **opinions** of mankind **requires** that they should **declare** the causes which **impel** them to the **separation**.

We hold these truths to be self-evident, that all men are **created** equal, that they are **endowed** by their **Creator** with certain unalienable Rights, that among these are Life, Liberty and the **pursuit** of Happiness. That to **secure** these rights, **Governments** are instituted among Men, **deriving** their just powers from the **consent** of the **governed**.

Reduced Vowels for Review

As a final review of this important chapter on stress and reduction, you will have an opportunity to break the habit of pronouncing each vowel fully, as you would in your native language. You must remind yourself that one of the most important factors to a great American accent is the concept of stress and reduction.

Read the word lists below, one row at a time, making sure that the vowel of the unstressed syllable is reduced and pronounced as /ə/, the schwa. The vowel spelling changes, but the vowel sound is the same in all of these groups of words.

A. Practice these words ending in ... /əl/				
	le	al	el	ul	ol
1.	little	social	level	awful	symbol
2.	gamble	mental	marvel	beautiful	idol
3.	able	final	travel	careful	capitol
4.	double	practical	angel	faithful	
5.	cycle	local	bagel	harmful	
6.	handle	animal	novel	thankful	

B. Practice these words ending in ... /ən/				
	an	en	on	ion
1.	ocean	fasten	common	fiction
2.	American	children	person	nation
3.	urban	chicken	lesson	million
4.	German	dozen	iron	direction
5.	woman	given	melon	attention
6.	veteran	driven	Jefferson	action

C. Practice these words ending in ... /ər/			
	ar	er	or	ure
1.	grammar	teacher	visitor	culture
2.	popular	driver	liquor	measure
3.	sugar	singer	actor	injure
4.	familiar	answer	color	future
5.	nuclear	sister	junior	failure
6.	regular	border	major	pressure

D. Practice these words ending in ... /əs/			
	ace	ous	ose	uce
1.	terrace	cautious	purpose	lettuce
2.	necklace	fabulous		
3.	palace	dangerous		
4.	grimace	curious		
5.	surface	delicious		
6.	preface	religious		

E. Practice these words ending in ... /ənt/		
	ant	ent
1.	distant	present
2.	elegant	accent
3.	infant	talent
4.	instant	frequent
5.	constant	document
6.	important	payment

Note: In this grouping of words the first syllables, rather than the last, are reduced.

F. Words beginning with... /ə/			
	a	e	o	u
1.	attain	enough	obtain	undo
2.	achieve	elect	object	unfit
3.	admit	effect	observe	untie
4.	adore	equip	obsess	unhappy
5.	awake	exam	offend	uncover
6.	announce	example	occur	unlock

Chapter Six

WORD STRESS

In this chapter you will learn the rules of stressing words within sentences. If you stress the right words your speech will have a natural rhythm and melody that is familiar to native speakers. The stress and reduction of words creates the music of English.

If your sentences are difficult to understand, it could be that you are not stressing *any* words, or else that you are stressing the *wrong* words. If you are not emphasizing any words, your speech will sound flat and monotone, and the listener will not know where one word begins and another ends. If you are stressing the wrong words, your speech will sound very foreign. For example, saying "I'll **see** you later." and "Have a **nice** day." sounds foreign to the American ear. Try changing the word stress and say: "I'll see you **later.**" and "Have a nice **day.**" Native speakers will recognize a familiar speech pattern this time and will be more likely to understand what you said, even if you are speaking quickly. So, if you have a tendency to speak too fast, learning to speak with correct word stress will automatically force you to slow down.

It's important to note that sometimes when the word stress changes, the meaning also changes. For example:

"I went to the white **house.**"
        or
"I went to the **White** House."

The first example describes a house that is white, while the second one is name of the place where the US President lives. Let's now learn some **rules** of word stress.

Compound Nouns

Compound nouns are two individual words that carry one meaning. They are part of one unit and have become a set phrase. Usually a compound noun consists of two nouns such as *credit + card*. In compound nouns, the first word is stressed, and the two words are said together, with no pausing in between the words. (Note that compound nouns can be written either as a single word or as two separate words.)

Compound Nouns for Practice

Stress the first word and pronounce the two words as one.

1. **parking** lot
2. **parking** ticket
3. **parking** meter
4. **parking** space

5. **book** shelf
6. **book** cover
7. **book** store
8. **book**mark

9. **credit** card
10. **post** card
11. **report** card
12. **green** card

13. **foot**ball
14. **base**ball
15. **ball**park
16. **ball**room

More Compound Noun Practice

Stress the first word in these compound nouns *within* compound nouns.

1. **cell** phone number
2. **foot**ball game
3. **bed**room furniture
4. **high** school girl

5. **basket**ball coach
6. **blood** pressure medicine
7. **web**site address
8. **parking** lot attendant

Words for Practice

These professions are all examples of compound nouns.

1. **taxi** driver
2. **computer** programmer
3. **real** estate **sales**person
4. **air**line pilot
5. **brain** surgeon

6. **research** scientist
7. **physician's** assistant
8. **math** teacher
9. **postal** worker
10. **high** school principal

Practice Dialogue

Leaving for Vacation

a. Hi Christine. Are you all packed?

b. I'm packing my **suit**case right now.

a. Did you remember to take everything?

b. Yes, I've got my **tooth**brush, **bathing** suit, **sun** block, **hair** dryer, **hair**spray, **air**line ticket, **running** shoes, **alarm** clock, and **credit** cards.

a. Don't forget the **telephone** number of the hotel. And **reading** material for the **air**plane. How are you getting to the **air**port?

b. The **taxi**cab will take me.

a. Do you have your **flight** information?

b. Yes, it's on the **airline** ticket and on the **boarding** pass. Uh oh. I forgot my **pass**port!

Practice Paragraph

At the Computer Store

I went to the **computer** store to buy a new computer. I couldn't decide between a **lap**top and a **desk**top. The **sales**man was very helpful. He told me all about the **hard** drives and the **operating** systems. I decided to get a **lap**top even though it has a smaller **key**board. He recommended a good **web**cam and a **flash** drive. I ended up also getting some **soft**ware, **head**phones, a **sound** card, and a **mouse** pad. I also got a **fax** machine, a few **video** games, and a **navigation** system for my car. But when I got to the **cash** register and gave them my **credit** card, they said I went over my **credit** limit. I was so embarrassed! I think I went **over**board!

Proper Stress with Adjectives

When an adjective is followed by a noun, the noun is stressed.

nice **day**   small **room**   blue **eyes**   old **man**

big **house**   long **time**   good **job**   first **grade**

When two adjectives precede a noun, stress the *first* adjective *and* the noun. The noun gets the most stress.

big blue **bus**   **nice** old **man**

really nice **day**   **cute** little **girl**

short black **hair**   **big** brown **eyes**

Practice Sentences

1. He's got big blue eyes and short black hair.
2. The nice young man helped the little old lady.
3. The big blue bus passed the little white car.
4. The rich young man bought that big old house.

Word Pairs for Practice

Practice saying the word pairs while stressing the words in bold letters.

Compound Noun	Adjective + Noun
1. **swimming** pool	deep **pool**
2. **drug** store	large **store**
3. **news**paper	new **paper**
4. **credit** card	plastic **card**
5. **sun**glasses	nice **glasses**
6. **post**man	tall **man**
7. **bus** driver	fast **driver**
8. **text**book	good **book**
9. **palm** tree	tall **tree**
10. **finger**nails	long **nails**
11. **girl**friend	great **friend**

Practice Sentences

1. They had a good **time** playing **foot**ball.
2. I bought some **sun**glasses at the new **store**.
3. My **hair**dresser has blond **hair**.
4. The **post**man brought me an important **letter**.
5. That **sales**man is a very nice **man**.
6. Her large **apartment** is on the third **floor** of that **apartment** building.
7. I left my **cell** phone in the front **seat** of my friend's **car**.
8. Let's go see the new **film** at the **movie** theater.

Compound Nouns Containing Adjectives

Sometimes in a compound noun, the first word is an adjective that no longer carries the original meaning. The meaning has been lost and has become a part of a fixed phrase or common expression. For example the adjective *super* in the compound noun *supermarket* doesn't make people think of the true meaning of the word *super*. Here are some other examples.

Words for Practice

1. **White** House
2. **green**house
3. **hot** dog
4. **blue** jeans
5. **high** school
6. **green** card
7. **dark**room
8. **cold** cut
9. **Blue**tooth
10. **high** rise

Phrasal Verbs

A "phrasal verb" is a verb + preposition combination that carries a special meaning. Phrasal verbs are idiomatic; they cannot be translated word-for-word. For example, *turn on, turn off, turn down,* and *turn up,* are all phrasal verbs. These types of words are very common in English and are often more frequently used than their one-word synonyms. For example, you are more likely to hear "**put out** the fire" rather than "**extinguish** the fire." In phrasal verbs, **the stress is on the last word**; note the bold words in the examples below.

phrasal verb	synonym
He *picked **up*** the box.	He *lifted* the box.
He *put **out*** his cigarette.	He *extinguished* his cigarette.
He *looked **over*** the material	He *reviewed* the material.

Practice Dialogues

Practice with *turn*

1. a. We don't need the heater.
    b. Turn it **off**. (stop, extinguish)
2. a. The music sounds good.
    b. Turn it **up**. (increase the volume)
3. a. Let's watch TV.
    b. Turn it **on**. (to light, to start)
4. a. He's impolite.
    b. That turns me **off**. (disgust)
5. a. The music is too loud.
    b. Turn it **down**. (decrease the volume)
6. a. Did he ask her out?
    b. She turned him **down**. (reject a request or a person)
7. a. He told me he'd be at the party.
    b. He didn't turn **up**. (appear, arrive)
8. a. Did you ask for help?
    b. They turned me **away**. (reject, refuse)

Noun Forms of Phrasal Verbs

Sometimes the phrasal verb has a noun equivalent, or a "phrasal noun." In that case, the stress is on the *first* word. We say "work **out**" if it's a verb, and "**work**out," if it's a noun.

Sentence Pairs for Practice

Phrasal verbs (stress on second word)	Nouns (stress on first word)
1. The car was tuned **up**.	My car needed a **tune**-up.
2. I worked **out** yesterday.	I had a great **work**out.
3. The papers were handed **out**.	We got some interesting **hand**outs.
4. They covered it **up** well.	I heard about the **cover**-up.
5. A lot of food was left **over**.	We ate **left**overs for lunch.
6. That really turns me **off**!	That's such a **turn**off!
7. They let me **down**.	It was a big **let**down.
8. The order was mixed **up**.	We're sorry about the **mix**-up.
9. He dropped **out**.	He's a high school **drop**out.
10. I need to sign **up** for the class.	Where is the **sign**-up sheet?

More Words for Practice

Stress the *first* word in these phrasal nouns within compound nouns.

1. **back**up plan
2. **cut**off date
3. **sign**-up sheet
4. **check**-out time
5. **warm**-up exercises
6. **pick**up truck
7. **carry**-on case
8. **play**-back button
9. **drop**-out rate
10. **work**out room
11. **stand**-up comedy
12. **drive**-through window
13. **sit**-down dinner
14. **make**up remover
15. **move** in date

Practice Sentences

Stress the highlighted words.

1. We have a **back**up plan in case things don't work **out**.
2. I found **out** that my **pick**up truck needs a **tune**-up.
3. The marriage was called **off** because the couple broke **up**.
4. Let's eat **out** after our **work**out.
5. He called me **up** to tell me about the **hold**up at the bank.
6. We dressed **up** for the **sit**-down dinner.
7. We found **out** that the **check**-in time was put **off**.
8. I am trying to cut **down** on eating **out**.
9. I looked it **over** and gave him the **print**out.
10. There was a **mix**-up at the **drive**-through window.

Abbreviations and Numbers

CD 3
Track
56

Always stress the last letter or the last number when pronouncing abbreviations.

Abbreviations for Practice

1. MB<u>A</u>
2. UCL<u>A</u>
3. JF<u>K</u>
4. CN<u>N</u>
5. US<u>A</u>
6. IB<u>M</u>
7. FB<u>I</u>
8. Ph<u>D</u>
9. AT&<u>T</u>

Numbers for Practice

1. 199<u>7</u>
2. 5:<u>15</u>
3. 11:<u>45</u>
4. $37.<u>99</u>
5. 91<u>1</u>
6. (31<u>0</u>) 55<u>5</u>- 238<u>9</u>

Practice Sentences

CD 3
Track
57

1. He arrived at LA<u>X</u> at 8:2<u>5</u> A<u>M</u>.
2. He has a Ph<u>D</u> from UCL<u>A</u>.
3. My SU<u>V</u> was made in the US<u>A</u>.
4. I love my IB<u>M</u> P<u>C</u>.
5. We arrived in the US<u>A</u> in 200<u>7</u>.
6. I bought the DV<u>D</u> player for $39.9<u>9</u>
7. My class starts and 9:<u>15</u> and ends at 10:<u>45</u>

Names of Places and People

CD 3
Track
58

When pronouncing a name—whether of a person or place—always stress the last word.

Place Names for Practice

1. New **York**
2. Central **Park**
3. South **Africa**
4. Venice **Beach**
5. Las **Vegas**
6. Palm **Springs**
7. North **Dakota**
8. Mount **Everest**

Names of People for Practice

1. George **Washington**
2. Bill **Clinton**
3. Tom **Cruise**
4. John F. **Kennedy**
5. Martin Luther **King**
6. Julia **Roberts**

Practice Paragraph

This passage includes examples of all of the different word stress rules you have learned so far. Stress the words in bold letters. The items you have studied in this chapter—such as compound nouns, names of people and places, phrasal verbs, abbreviations—are in italics.

Trip to LA

I am planning to visit the *West Coast*. I will take *United Airlines* flight *307*. It leaves *JFK* at *9:00 am* and arrives at *LAX* at *12:15*. I *found out* that there's a **three** hour **time** **difference** between *LA* and *New York*. I hope I *get over* my **jetlag** pretty quickly. After I *check in* at the hotel, I will call a **taxicab** to *pick me up* and take me to *Universal Studios*. Who knows, I might even see some famous **movie** stars like *Tom Cruise* and *Brad Pitt*. Oh, I hope I don't *pass out*! I also plan to visit *Palm Springs* and *San Diego*. On my way **back**, I'm planning a **layover** in *Las Vegas*. I really think it's going to be a nice **getaway**.

Word Stress Within a Sentence

You will now learn the rules of stress and reduction within sentences. First let's learn *how* words should sound when they are stressed. For now, just keep in mind that we generally stress words that carry the most meaning.

Lengthening the Main Vowel in Stressed Words

When the stressed word has only one syllable, just prolong the word and make the vowel higher in pitch. If the stressed word has more than one syllable, make sure that the stressed syllable of the word is prolonged and emphasized more than usual.

Prolonging the stressed vowel may sound exaggerated to you, particularly if the vowel is already a long vowel, such as /a/ and /ae/ and /ou/. For example, if you say, "It's really f**a**r." or "St**o**p that!," the vowel sound may be much longer than it would sound in your native language. Don't say: "It's really far." Say: "It's really *far (faaar)*." Don't say "Stop that!" Say "*Stop (staaap)* that!" Let's first get used to prolonging the vowels within stressed words since this will create a distinctly American sound to your English.

Practice with Vowel Length

Make sure you raise your pitch and prolong the underlined vowel in the stressed words below.

Stressed Words with /ɑ/

1. I **g_o_t** it.
2. I **g_o_t** a new j**o**b.
3. I think I **g_o_t** a new **j_o_b**.

Stressed Words with /æ/

1. I have a new **cl_a_ss**.
2. I can't **st_a_nd** it.
3. I can't st**a**nd my new **cl_a_ss**.
4. I'll call you **b_a_ck**.
5. …as soon as I **c_a_n**.
6. I'll call you **b_a_ck** as soon as I **c_a_n**.

Stressed words with /ou/

1. It's so **c<u>o</u>ld**.
2. I didn't **kn<u>ow</u>**.
3. I didn't **kn<u>ow</u>** about it.
4. I didn't **kn<u>ow</u>** it would be so **c<u>o</u>ld**.

Stressed words with /i/

1. How do you **f<u>ee</u>l**?
2. When did he **l<u>ea</u>ve**?
3. How did you **f<u>ee</u>l** when he had to **l<u>ea</u>ve**?

Stressed words with /ɔ/

1. That's **<u>aw</u>ful**.
2. It's too **l<u>o</u>ng**.
3. That **<u>aw</u>ful** n<u>o</u>vel is too **l<u>o</u>ng**.
4. I'm **exh<u>au</u>sted**.
5. I've been **t<u>a</u>lking** all day **l<u>o</u>ng**.
6. I'm **exh<u>au</u>sted** from **t<u>a</u>lking <u>a</u>ll** day **l<u>o</u>ng**.

Advice from a Successful Student

"I record myself reading in English. I listen to the recordings and write down the mistakes. This way, I catch the sounds that I don't normally catch when I am speaking with people."

Mai Ling, China

Which Words Should I Stress?

CD 3 Track 64

Now that you have had a quick introduction to *how* words sound when they are stressed and reduced, let's learn the rules of which words are stressed and which are reduced.

Content Words

"Content words" are the words that carry the most meaning. These words are usually nouns, verbs, adjectives, adverbs, and sometimes question words such as *when, why,* or *where*. If we removed the surrounding words and just spoke using content words, the general idea of what we were trying to say would still be understood. For example, imagine that you heard someone say: "Went store morning." You would understand that they meant: "I went to the store in the morning."

Also, content words are like key words that you would use when searching a topic on the internet. For example, you would only type: "SYMPTOMS, HEART ATTACK," instead of "What are the symptoms of a heart attack?" Another good example of content words can be found in newspaper headlines. They would say: "Suspect arrested" instead of "A suspect has been arrested;"and "Neighbors complain" instead of "The neighbors have been complaining."

As a general rule, the **last** content word of a phrase gets the most stress. So, in the sentence "A suspect has been arrested," *arrested* will get the most stress. Similarly, we don't say: "The **neighbors** have been complaining." Instead, we stress the last content word and we say: "The neighbors have been **complaining**."

Now let's practice stressing content words and placing the most stress on the final content word.

Practice Sentences

Remember to stress the last content word in each sentence. Notice how the stress changes as more information is added to the end. The underlined word gets the most stress.

1. I like **bacon**.
   I like **bacon** and <u>**eggs**</u>.

2. It's **black**.
   It's **black** and <u>**white**</u>.

3. Do you want **salt**?
   Do you want **salt** and <u>**pepper**</u>?

4. That's **good**.
   That's a good <u>**idea**</u>.

5. It's **hot**.
   It's a hot <u>**day**</u>.

6. I **need** it.
   I need to <u>**go**</u>.
   I need to **go** <u>**home**</u>.
   I need to go **home** at five <u>**o'clock**</u>.

7. I **saw** him.
   I saw the **man**.
   I saw the **man** you <u>**told**</u> me about.*

*Note: *me* and *about* are not stressed because they are not content words.

8. He **drove** it.
   He **drove** the **car**.
   He **drove** the **car** he <u>**bought**</u> yesterday.
   He **drove** the **car** that he **bought** from his <u>**friend**</u>.

Content Words in Detail: Verbs

Verbs are action words, such as *go*, *eat*, and *study*. We emphasize main verbs more than the participles or gerunds that come before them. That's because words like *can*, *could*, *am*, *been*, *don't*, and *have* (when it's a participle) are less important than the main verb.

Practice Sentences

Notice how the verbs are stressed the most and how the surrounding words have been reduced.

1. I'll **call** you.
2. I **saw** him.
3. I'll **wait** for you.
4. I **have** to **go**.
5. It's nice to **meet** you.

Stress Nouns but Not Pronouns

We stress nouns like *man, book, John,* and *Mary.* We don't stress pronouns such as *he, it, her,* and *myself.*

Practice Sentences

stressed nouns:
1. He told **John**.
2. I like that **car**.
3. I need a **job**.

reduced pronouns:
He **told** him.
I **like** it.
I **need** it.

Content Words in Detail: Adjectives

Place full stress on an adjective if it's not followed by a noun. If it is followed by a noun, stress the noun more.

adjective alone:
1. That was **good**.
2. It's really **hot**.
3. It's **long**.
4. John is **nice**.

adjective + noun:
That was a **good** <u>film</u>.
It's a really **hot** <u>day</u>.
It's a **long** <u>drive</u>.
John is a **nice** <u>man</u>.

Practice Sentences

A.
1. **Wait!**
2. I'll **wait** for you.
3. I can **wait** for you.
4. I am **waiting** for you.
5. I'll be **waiting** for you.
6. I've been **waiting** for you.
7. I could've **waited** for you.
8. I could've been **waiting** for you.
9. I'll **wait** for you in the **car**.
10. I should've been **waiting** for you in the **car**.

B.

1. **Tell** her.
2. He'll **tell** her.
3. He'll be **telling** her.
4. He didn't **tell** her.
5. He should have **told** her.
6. He should've been **telling** her.
7. He didn't **tell** his **wife**.
8. He should've been **telling** his **wife**.
9. He didn't **tell** his **wife** about the **situation**.
10. He should've been **telling** his **wife** about the **situation**.

C.

1. I **bought** it.
2. I **bought** a **watch**.
3. I **bought** a new **watch**.
4. I **bought** a new gold **watch**.
5. I **bought** a new gold **watch** for him.
6. I **bought** a new gold **watch** for his **birthday**.
7. I **bought** a new gold **watch** for his thirtieth **birthday**.
8. I would have **bought** a new gold **watch** for his thirtieth **birthday**.

D.

1. He **lost** it.
2. He **lost** the **money**.
3. I **think** he **lost** the **money**.
4. I **think** he **lost** the **money** again.
5. I **think** he **lost** the **money** that I **gave** him.
6. He might have **lost** the **money** that I **gave** him.
7. I **think** he might have **lost** the **money** that I **gave** him.

Reducing Vowels in Unstressed Words

We reduce "function words." These types of words generally don't carry as much importance or meaning as the content words. If they were eliminated, the sentence would still make sense. Here is a list of the function words:

a. **pronouns** - *he, she, you, they, mine, his, himself,* etc.
b. **prepositions** - *to, in, for, at, by, on, with, from,* etc.
c. **conjunctions** - *and, but, or, nor, so, yet*
d. **auxiliary verbs** - *am, is, was, were, do, does, been, have, can, could, should,* etc.
e. **articles** – *a, an, the*
f. **indefinite pronouns** - *one, some, any, anywhere, somewhere, anything, something,* etc.

There is one exception to the rule above: auxiliary verbs are stressed in their negative forms. See below.

affirmative:	*negative:*
I can **do** it.	I **can't do** it.
He should **try** it.	He **shouldn't try** it.
I'd **like** it.	I **wouldn't like** it.

Weak Forms

When a word is reduced we use the "weak form" of the word. The weak form is said more quickly and more softly. The vowel becomes the schwa sound, /ə/. For example, the preposition *for* sounds like "fur" or /fər/, and *at* sounds like /ət/. Let's now practice using the weak forms of some commonly unstressed words.

Practice Sentences

to becomes /tə/

1. I'd like *to* go.
2. I need *to* talk *to* you.
3. I'd like *to* go *to* the park.

and becomes /n/

1. bacon *'n'* eggs
2. black *'n'* white
3. in *'n'* out
4. rock *'n'* roll

for becomes /fər/

1. Let's go *for* a walk.
2. Wait *for* John.
3. This is *for* Bill.
4. I'm looking *for* my book.

can becomes /kən/

1. I *can* do it.
2. You *can* call me.
3. *Can* you swim?
4. When *can* you come over?

as becomes /əz/

1. It's *as* big *as* a house.
2. I'm *as* hungry *as* a wolf.
3. I'll call you *as* soon *as* I can.
4. Keep it *as* long *as* you need it.

or becomes /ər/

1. Is it this one *or* that one?
2. I'll do it today *or* tomorrow.
3. I saw it five *or* six times.
4. I'm leaving on Monday *or* Tuesday.

Strong Forms

When the function word is at the end of the sentence, or if it's used for emphasis, make sure you use the "strong form" of the word. Let's compare a few sentences with weak and strong forms.

	weak form *reduced vowel*	*strong form* *full vowel*
for	/fər/ I'm looking *for* you.	Who are you looking **for**?
to	/tə/ Would you like *to* go?	I'd love **to**.
at	/ət/ He's *at* the bank.	Are you laughing **with** me or **at** me?

Practice Dialogues

1. Reducing *yourself, myself*

a. I'm really **ashamed** of *myself*.
b. You need to **forgive** *yourself* and **tell** *yourself* that everyone makes mistakes. Stop **punishing** *yourself*. Otherwise, you'll **drive** *yourself* crazy. Why do you **doubt** *yourself* so much?
a. I guess I can't **help** *myself*.

2. Reducing *anywhere, anyone, anything*

a. How was your weekend? Did you **do** *anything* interesting?
b. I didn't **do** *anything*, I didn't **see** *anyone*, I didn't **go** *anywhere*.

3. Reducing *to, for, as, of, can, an*

a. Are you the **owner** *of* this **restaurant**?
b. Yes I **am**.
a. *Can* I **talk** *to* you *for* a **moment**?
b. Sure, how *can* I **help** you?
a. We've been **waiting** *for* our **food** *for* over *an* **hour**.
b. I'm sorry *for* the **delay**. I'll talk *to* the **chef** and I'll bring it **out** *as* soon *as* I **can**.

Thought Groups and Focus Words

When sentences are longer, they are divided into "thought groups." Thought groups are words that naturally belong together as a grammatical unit. We instinctively pause between thought groups, although the pause is not as long as when there's a comma or a period.

Here is an example of a sentence that is divided into two different thought groups:

"I like bacon and eggs ///early in the morning." It's natural to divide this sentence, and it sounds better than if you had said: "I like bacon and eggs early in the morning," without pausing.

Within each thought group there is always one word that gets the most stress. That stressed word is called a "focus word." The focus word is the word that carries the key information of the thought group. It's usually the last content word within the thought group. For example, in the example sentence above, *eggs* and *morning* are the focus words.

There is some variation between different speakers regarding how often to pause within a longer sentence. People who speak quickly tend to pause less and their sentences have fewer thought groups.

Practice Sentences

Practice stressing the focus words and pausing between the thought groups.

1. I want to **talk** to you // about something **important**.
2. If you give me your **email** address, */ / I will send you the **information**.
3. Every time I stop by his **office**, // he's too busy to **talk** to me.
4. I wonder how **long** // it will **take** me //to learn to speak **English** like you.
5. What did you think of the new **restaurant** // that we **went** to last night?
6. He has been looking for a new **job** // for a long **time** now // but he just hasn't **found** anything // that he really **likes**.

(*Email address* is a compound noun, so we stress the first word.)

Practice Conversations: Telephone Messages

Practice these voicemail messages using correct word stress. The focus word of each thought group is in bold letters. The thought groups are divided by slashes.

A. Phone Tag

Mary's Answering Machine: Hi, this is **Mary**. I am **sorry** // I missed your **call**. Please leave a **message** // after the **beep**, and I'll call you **back** // as soon as I **can**.

Mike: Hi **Mary**, this is **Mike**. It's been a **while** // since we last **spoke**. I hope you're **doing** well. I'm calling to **see** // if you're **free** tomorrow. I am going **hiking** // with some **friends** // and I wanted to **see** // if you'd like to **join** us. It would be great to **see** you. Give me a **call** // and let me **know** // if you're **available**.

Mary: Hi **Mike**, this is **Mary**, returning your **call**. It was great to **hear** from you. Sorry that we keep **missing** each other. Yeah, I'd love to go **hiking** with you. Let me **know** // what time you're thinking of **going**. I'm looking **forward** to it. I should be home **tonight** // after **seven**, so **call** me // and let me **know** // where we should **meet**.

B. Sales Call

Note that individual speaking style or some circumstances can determine the number of thought groups there are in a sentence. For example, the following speech has fewer thought groups because the speaker is a salesman who needs to deliver his message quickly.

Good **afternoon**, Mr. **Johnson**. This is Bill **Jones** calling. I would like to **tell** you about the new **product** // our **company** is selling. I **believe** // it will greatly benefit your **organization**. We recently conducted a **study** // on how your customer's **needs** are changing. We are able to help you run your business more **efficiently** // and at the same **time**, save you **money**. I think that people in your **firm** // would be very interested in our **services**. I'd like to set up a time to **talk** with you // about how our company can **help** you. I can **assure** you // that it will be worth your **while**. When would be a good **time** // for us to **meet**?

Contrastive Stress

> *Be nice to **people** // on your way __up__ // because you might*
> *__meet__ them // on the way __down__.*
> Wilson Mizner

We also sometimes stress words to bring out a special meaning or to clarify what we mean when there is confusion. In this case, *any* word in a sentence can be stressed, including a function word.

Practice Sentences

Each of the following sentences can be stressed in four different ways, depending on the meaning that the speaker wants to convey.

1.

	implied meaning:
I don't love him.	*….but she does*
I **don't** love him.	*I really don't.*
I don't **love** him.	*But I think he's a nice person.*
I don't love **him**.	*But I love the other guy.*

2.

	implied meaning:
I may drive to New York.	*Not she.*
I **may** drive to New York.	*Maybe, I'm not sure.*
I may **drive** to New York.	*Not fly.*
I may drive to **New York**.	*Not Boston.*

Contrastive Stress for Clarification

> **What lies behind us and what lies before us are tiny matters compared to what lies within us.**
> *Oliver Wendell Holmes*

Notice how the stressed words emphasize a particular meaning or a need for clarification.

1. Do you need a ticket **to** Paris or **from** Paris?
2. Did you say **in**side or **out**side?
3. I want **two** pieces, not **one**.
4. It's **under** the desk, not **on** the desk.
5. The government is **of** the people, **by** the people, and **for** the people.

Emphasizing Auxiliaries

Notice the extra stress placed on the auxiliaries to clarify or strengthen a point. The underlined word indicates extra stress.

1. a. You don't **understand** me.
   b. I **do** **understand** you.

2. a. You didn't **go**, did you?
   b. I **did** **go**.

3. a. It's **hot** isn't it?
   b. It **is** hot.

4. a. You've never **been** here, have you?
   b. I **have** been here.

Practice Dialogue

Making an Appointment

a. Hello, **dentist's** office.

b. I'm **calling** // to make an **appointment** // for a **dental** checkup.

a. I have an **opening** // on **Tuesday** // at 5 **pm**.

b. I'll have to **work** late // on that **day**. Do you **have** anything // on Friday **morning**?

a. I don't **have** anything // on Friday **morning**, but I <u>do</u> have // Friday <u>afternoon</u>.

b. Hmm, let me **check**. I <u>think</u> I can make it. Yes, I **can**. I <u>can</u> **make** it.

a. Would you like <u>three</u> o'clock or <u>four</u> o'clock?

b. <u>Four</u> o'clock sounds **good**.

a. Will this be your first **visit** // to our **office**?

b. No, it'll be my <u>second</u> visit.

Chapter Seven

INTONATION

"Intonation" is the melody of language and is made up of pitches that rise and fall. This rising and falling melody is used to communicate our intentions and our emotions. In spoken language, intonation replaces punctuation. It tells the listener whether we are finished talking or whether we have something more to say; whether we are asking a question or making a statement. Intonation also gives information that words alone cannot give. It can indicate anger, surprise, confusion, hesitation, sarcasm, interest, or lack of interest. If your speech has good intonation it will be more dynamic and more interesting to listen to.

Falling Intonation

Lower your voice at the end of the sentence to produce a "falling intonation." This intonation is used for a variety of reasons:

Statements

Falling intonation is used in simple sentences that are not questions. For example:

1. My name is John.

2. It's nice to meet you.

3. Have a nice day.

4. I'm going outside.

5. I'll be back in a minute.

Questions

Falling intonation is also used when asking questions if they contain interrogative words such as *where, what, why, when, how,* and *who.* For example:

1. What's his name?

2. Why did you leave?

3. Where are you going?

4. What are you thinking about?

5. How are you doing?

6. When does it start?

7. Who told you?

Rising Intonation

Raise the pitch of your voice at the end of a sentence to create "rising intonation." Rising intonation is used in "yes/no questions." For example, "Did you see it?" is a "yes/no" question. It can be answered with either a "yes" or a "no." Compare that question with this one: "When did you see it?" this one cannot be answered by a simple "yes" or "no."

Practice Sentences

1. Did he work yesterday?

2. Does he know about it?

3. Can you call me at five?

4. Is it good?

5. Is that it?

6. Excuse me?

7. Really?

Advice from a Successful Student

"I don't get upset with myself if my accent isn't perfect. I know I am making progress as long as I practice all the time. Don't be too hard on yourself if you are still making mistakes. Developing an American accent is a process. It doesn't happen overnight."

Sabrina Stoll, Germany

Sentence Pairs for Practice

The following question pairs contain both rising and falling intonation, depending on whether they contain a "question word" or whether they are "yes/no" questions. The first question of the pair has rising intonation, and the second has falling intonation.

yes/no question	question words
1. Do you teach?	What do you teach?
2. Did you see the movie?	When did you see the movie?
3. Do you know that guy?	How do you know that guy?
4. Did you buy the car?	Where did you buy the car?
5. Do you work there?	Why do you work there?

Non-final Intonation

With "non-final intonation," the pitch rises and falls within the sentence or word. This type of intonation is used in various situations which are outlined below.

Unfinished Thoughts

Non-final intonation is often used to indicate that you have not ended a thought. To indicate that you have something more to say, raise your pitch at the end of the phrase. For example, "When I saw him..." or "If I study hard..."

Sentence Pairs for Practice

The first sentence in each pair has falling intonation which indicates that the thought has ended. The second sentence contains rising intonation indicating that the thought has not ended.

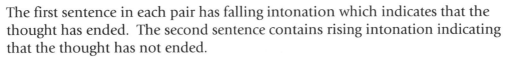

1. I bought the book.	I bought the book, but I didn't read it.
2. I finished school.	When I finished school, I moved to New York.
3. I'll study hard.	If I study hard, I'll get an A.
4. I'm going inside.	I'm going inside, to get something to drink.

Introductory Words

Non-final intonation is also used with introductory words, such as *actually* or *by the way*. Since these types of words indicate that a thought is not finished, the non-final intonation is appropriate.

Practice Sentences

1. As a matter of fact, I do know the answer.

2. As far as I'm concerned, you did great.

3. Actually, it was pretty good.

4. In my opinion, it's too expensive.

5. If you don't mind, I'd like to close the window.

6. By the way, how did you know that?

Series of Words

Non-final intonation is used in words and phrases that are listed in a series. The voice rises at the end of each item, but falls with the final item.

Practice Sentences

1. I like football, basketball, tennis, and golf.

2. I'm taking math, biology, French, and history.

3. I left work, came home, and had dinner.

4. I need milk, apples, eggs, and sugar.

5. "I learned law so well, the day I graduated I sued the college, won the case, and

   got my tuition back." ~Fred Allen

Expressing Choices

Finally, non-final intonation is used when giving a choice between two or more things.

1. Do you want to eat in or eat out?

2. Is your birthday in March or in April?

3. Do you speak Cantonese or Mandarin?

4. Is his name Matthew or Michael?

5. Do you want the blue one or the black one?

Wavering Intonation

"Wavering intonation" is used for expressing specific emotions or attitudes. With this type of intonation, the pitch changes within words.

Some of the emotions you can express with your intonation include anger, surprise, sarcasm, hesitation, uncertainty, disgust, fear, amazement, and pity.

Let's start with the words *you did*. We can say them five different ways depending on the emotion or intention. Listen to the audio to hear the intonation changes.

	Meaning
1. You did?	*curious*
2. You did?	*very surprised*
3. You did?	*disappointed*
4. You did?	*angry*
5. You did.	*in agreement*

Now try saying the expression, *thanks a lot*, in three different ways. Change the intonation each time.

1. Thanks a lot.	*normal*
2. Thanks a lot.	*very happy*
3. Thanks a lot.	*sarcastic*

Try saying *okay* with different emotions.

Okay.	*normal*
Okay.	*hesitant or unwilling*
Okay!	*very excited*
Okay!	*frustrated and angry*

Try saying *no* with different emotions.

No!	*angry*
No?	*surprised*
No...	*hesitant*
No.	*sarcastic*

Practice Dialogues

Angry Friends

a. Did you do it?	*curious*
b. No.	*normal*
a. No?	*very surprised*
b. No!	*angry*
a. Why not?	*surprised*
b. I don't know.	*hesitant*
a. You don't know?	*angry*
b. I don't know.	*angry*
a. Oh really?	*sarcastic*
b. Yeah, really.	*angry*

Losing Weight

This dialogue has examples of all of the types of intonation you have learned so far.

Emily: Rachel, is that you?

Rachel: Hi Emily.

Emily: I didn't recognize you at first. Did you lose weight?

Rachel: As a matter of fact, I lost twenty pounds.

Emily: Really? How did you do it?

Rachel: Well, I stopped eating cake, ice cream, potato chips, and candy bars, and I started eating healthier foods like salads, fruit, nuts, and vegetables.

Emily: Wow! I have to say, you look amazing.

Rachel: Do you really think so?

Emily: Absolutely!

Chapter Eight

SOUND LIKE A TRUE NATIVE SPEAKER

This chapter will share some important information that will help you sound more like a true native speaker. You will learn the rules of how words are connected together so that your speech flows better and sounds more natural and more fluent. You will also learn more about which words to reduce and exactly how to reduce them. And you will learn the differences between casual, relaxed speech and more formal, careful speech.

Linking Words for Smoother Speech Flow

Many non-native speakers of English believe they should pronounce each word separately because they want to make sure their speech is clear and easily understood. This does help their speech sound clear, but it also creates speech that sounds a bit foreign and a bit mechanical, almost like computer-generated speech.

Native speakers connect, or "link," words together if the words are part of the same thought group. They connect the last sound of one word to the first sound of the next word. Linking creates the smooth, uninterrupted sounds that are they key to natural, fluent sounding speech.

If you're making the common error of dropping the endings of words by not pronouncing the final consonant, the problem will automatically be solved when you apply the rules of linking to your speech. Linking requires you to connect the final consonant with the next word, if it begins with a vowel. In this way, the final sound, which is always more difficult to pronounce, becomes the first sound of the word that follows it. For example, it's more difficult to say "burn**ed** out" than to say "burn doubt."

Instead of saying "it's - a - cold - evening" with each word pronounced separately, say "it sa col devening," and your speech will instantly sound more native-like and you are guaranteed to pronounce the final consonants.

⚠ Warning: Common Mistake

Linking and speaking fast are *not* the same thing! You don't need to speak fast. When native speakers link words, they are not necessarily speaking faster. The speech is just smoother, and less choppy. It's extremely important to stress the content words when you are linking words because this will force you to slow down at the right place, and it will make your speech more easily understood.

CD 4
Track
21

Rules for Linking

Linking Consonant to Vowel

When a word ends in a consonant and the next word begins with a vowel, connect the final consonant to the next vowel, making it sound as if the second word starts with a consonant. Study the examples below to make this point clear.

	sounds like:
1. hold on	"whole Don"
2. I like it	"I lie kit"
3. deep end	"depend"
4. get up late	"get a plate"
5. picked out	"pick doubt"
6. this guy	"the sky"

CD 4
Track
22

Practice Dialogues

Note that the words in bold get the most stress.

1. a. Can‿I come‿**in**?

   b. Yes, come‿**on**‿in. The door‿is‿**open**.

2. a. Should‿I leave‿it‿**on**?

   b. No, turn‿it‿**off**.

3. a. What **time**‿is‿it?

   b. It's‿**already** five‿**o'clock**.

4. a. Let's take a **walk**.

b. That's a good **idea**.

5. a. How **far** is it?

b. **Four** and a half **hours** away.

6. a. This is a good **film**.

b. Too bad it's sold **out**.

7. a. I have an awful **headache**.

b. Take an **aspirin**.

8. a. This is my brother-in-**law**.

b. We've already **met**.

Linking Consonant to Same Consonant

When the final consonant of one word is the same as the first consonant of the following word, pronounce the consonant only once. Do not pause between the sounds, but just lengthen the sound a bit or say it with a little bit more energy. See the example below.

	sounds like:
1. She speaks Spanish.	"She speak Spanish."
2. turned down	"turn down"
3. help Paul	help all
4. well lit	well it
5. black cat	black at
6. foreign name	foreign aim

Word Pairs for Practice

1. big game
2. well lit
3. can never
4. good day
5. this Saturday

6. far right
7. stop playing
8. Tom might
9. book club
10. what time

Practice Sentences

1. Both things are from me.
2. Stop playing and help Paul.
3. She's single and she's so happy.
4. I'm married and I'm miserable.
5. It was so nice to meet Tom.

Final Stop Between Consonants

In Chapter Three you learned the difference between stops and continuants. Remember, when a stop is followed by another consonant, do not release the stop. The release creates a puff of air and an extra syllable. Make sure that *good time* doesn't sound like "good a time" and that *help me* doesn't sound like "help a me."

Word Pairs for Practice

1. pop music
2. good book
3. can't go
4. that man
5. drop down
6. keep trying

Linking Vowel to Vowel

If one word ends with a vowel and the next word begins with a vowel, do not pause between the words. For a smoother transition between the sounds and to ensure a complete pronunciation of both of the vowels, we insert a short /w/ sound after a front vowel (such as /eɪ/, /i/, and /ai/) and a short /y/ sound after a back vowel (such as /ʊ/ and /oʊ/) .

		Sounds like:
Insert a very quick /w/ sound	go out	"go – wout"
	How are you?	"how ware you"
Insert a very quick /y/ sound	I am	"I yam"
	they are	"they yare"

Practice Sentences

1. I ʸate out.
2. Go ʷon.
3. They ʸagree.
4. I know ʷit.

5. May ʸI come in?
6. So ʷawesome!
7. I'll buy ʸit.
8. He ʸate out.

Practice Dialogues

1. a. Why ʸare you so ʷupset?

   b. I ʸam not!

2. a. Who ʷis he?

   b. He ʸis the ʸannouncer.

3. a. How ʷis the weather?

   b. Go ʷoutside and find out.

4. Do ʷI need to do ʷit?

   No, I ʸalready did it.

Do I Say *the* or *thee*?

When the article *the* is followed by a vowel sound, it is pronounced with /i/ and sounds like "thee." When it is followed by a consonant, the final sound is /ə/, like the *u* in *fun*.

/i/	/ə/
the earth	the world

/i/	/ə/
the apple	the banana

Linking Vowels Within a Word

When an individual word contains two vowel sounds together, we also add a little *y* or *w* sound. We don't say "die it" we say "die + yet."

Word Pairs for Practice

	sounds like:		*sounds like:*
client	"cli /y/ ent"	cooperate	"co /w/ operate"
science	"sci /y/ ence"	experience	"experi /y/ ence"
serious	"seri /y/ ous"	diet	"di /y/ et"
quiet	"qui /y/ et"	furious	"furi /y/ ous"
appreciate	"appreci/y/ate"	negotiate	"negoci/y/ate"
museum	"muse/y/um"	San Diego	"San Di /y/ago"

Practice Dialogue

This exercise and those that follow will help you practice linking. Remember to place the most stress on the key word, usually a noun or a verb. For longer sentences place the most stress on the focus word of each thought group.

In the Department Store

a. Can I help you?

b. I'm looking for a pair of sunglasses.

a. The sunglasses are on the other side of the make up counter.

b. Oh these are nice. Can I try them on?

a. The mirror is over here.

b. How much are these?

a. They're on sale for one hundred and eighty dollars.

b. That's a lot of money. I don't think I can afford that.

a. The style is amazing. We're almost all sold out.

a. Do you have any that are cheaper?

b. No, I am afraid I don't. Is there anything else I can help you find?

a. As a matter of fact, yes. Help me find a rich husband!

More Practice Dialogues

Notice how two same or similar consonants blend into one to link words more smoothly. The final stops are not released.

1. a. I believe‿Veronica speaks‿Spanish.
   b. Of course‿she does. She's from‿Mexico.
   a. That makes‿sense.

2. a. When's the big‿game?
   b. Either this‿Saturday or this‿Sunday.
   a. Do you think they'll‿lose?
   b. I hope not.

3. a. Keep‿practicing.
   b. You're‿right, I need‿to.

4. a. You'll‿love it.
   b. I suppose‿so.

5. a. It was a fun‿night but I need‿to go.
   b. Let's‿stay a little‿longer.
   a. You stay, I'll‿leave with‿them.
   b. Okay then, I'll‿leave too.

Practice Paragraph

This passage provides practice in linking vowel to vowel, consonant to vowel, and consonant to consonant. The focus words are in bold letters. The thought groups are divided by a slash.

My American Accent

I've been practicing the ʸAmerican‿**accent** // for‿a **while** now. At **first**, // it was kind‿of **hard** // to keep **track**‿of‿all the rules‿and‿**exceptions**. I had no ʷ**idea** // there was‿so much to **learn**. I've been **practicing** // with the ʸ**audio** materials. // It's‿ somewhat‿**easier** // to pronounce‿some‿of the **sounds** // but‿it's difficult to **know** // how ʷI sound‿to ʷ**others**. I think I'm getting **better**. One‿of the hardest‿**things** for me // is to stress‿some **syllables** // and to reduce‿certain‿**others**. When‿I ʸask my **friends** // how ʷI **sound**, they ʸall **say** // they hear‿a difference‿in my **speech**. My **boss**‿said // that‿I am‿making **progress** // and that‿I **sound** // more‿and more like‿a native **speaker**. My clients‿are not‿**asking** me // to **repeat** myself‿as much. It makes‿it‿all **worthwhile**. I won'**t** stop‿**practicing**.

Warning: Common Mistake

Don't pause within thought groups.

Don't say:
He's // at work until eleven // o'clock.

Say:
He's at work // until eleven o'clock.

Reducing Pronouns

In the chapter on word stress you learned that pronouns are not stressed. When we reduce the pronouns, the first letter is often silent. For example, the letter *h* is often silent for the words *he*, *him*, *his*, *her*, and *hers* when these pronouns are not the first words of a sentence. Also, the *th* sound is often silent for the word *them*. This is particularly true in casual speech, but it frequently occurs in formal speech as well. Study the example below.

	sounds like:
1. I love her	"I lover"
2. I knew her	"I newer"
3. stuff he knows	"stuffy nose"
4. did he	"didee"
5. has he	"hazee"

Note: Always pronounce the first consonant of a pronoun when the pronoun is in the beginning of a sentence or a phrase.

Practice Dialogues

Remember that the *h* in *he* and *him* is silent except when these words begin the sentence.

The New Boyfriend

Is *he* nice?
What's *his* name?
What does *he* look like?
How old is *he*?
Where does *he* live?
What does *he* do?
How long have you known *him*?
Do you love *him*?
Where's *his* family from?
When can we meet *him*?
Did you tell *him* we'd like to meet him?
What did *he* say?
Answer: He said that *he* thinks my friends ask too many questions!

Who's Laura Jones?

Now you will practice the silent *h* of the pronoun *her*.

a. Do you know Laura Jones?
b. Yeah, I know *her*.
a. How do you know *her*?
b. I know *her* from school.
a. Have you seen *her* lately?
b. I just saw *her* a few days ago. I see *her* about twice a week. She has *her* dance class next door to mine.
a. Next time you see *her*, tell *her* I want to talk to *her*.

All About Eggs

The *th* of the pronoun *them* is silent in these sentences.

a. I love eggs.
b. How do you cook *them*?
a. All sorts of ways. I boil *them*, I fry *them*, I scramble *them*, and I poach *them*.
b. Do you just eat *them* for breakfast?
a. No, I have *them* for dinner too. I cut *them* up and put *them* in salads.

Study Tip

When you watch an American film, try to watch it with closed captioning or subtitles in English. This is a very useful method for developing better listening skills, using the right melody and learning the common reductions of American speech. Play back some scenes and repeat the actors' lines several times until you can say them the same way.

Contractions

A "contraction" is a word that is made shorter when it is linked to the word that comes before it. For example, "**she is** nice." is usually contracted to "**she's** nice." Contractions are a standard part of English speech and they're used even in very formal situations. Using contractions is not considered sloppy or lazy speech. In fact, if you don't use contractions, your speech will sound mechanical and foreign and might even give the impression that you are not very fluent in English. For example, you will hear people say, "**I'm** happy," rather than "**I am** happy." If you do hear "I **am** happy" it's usually in response to an opposite statement or question, such as "I don't think you're happy." If the response is "I **am** happy!" with stress on the word *am*, the meaning is "I *really* am happy."

Another situation in which a contraction may not be used is when a speaker pauses in order to think of what to say next. For example: "I am… happy."

Note: Do not use contractions in written language, unless the writing is informal.

Commonly Contracted Words

1. **The Verb** *to be*

   I'm happy.
   She's American.

2. **Auxiliary Verbs**
   These include *be, would, will,* and *have.*

   He's working.
   He'd like to go.
   I'll call you.
   I've been there.

3. **The Word** *not*
   Not is contracted when it follows *have, be, can, could, should, would,* and *must.*

   I **haven't** been there.
   I **can't** do that.

Practice with Contractions: will

1. I will do it.	**I'll** do it.
2. You will like it.	**You'll** like it.
3. He will call you.	**He'll** call you.
4. We will take it.	**We'll** take it.
5. They will see.	**They'll** see.
6. It will rain.	**It'll** rain.
7. It will be good.	**It'll** be good.
8. That will be all.	**That'll** be all.
9. There will be snow.	**There'll** be snow.

Practice with Contractions: would

1. I would go.   **I'd** go.
2. I would like some more.   **I'd** like some more.
3. He would go if he could.   **He'd** go if he could.
4. She would understand.   **She'd** understand.
5. We would like to see it.   **We'd** like to see it.

Practice with Contractions: had

Note that this contraction sounds the same as the contraction of *would*.

1. I had never seen it before.   **I'd** never seen it before.
2. She had known about it.   **She'd** known about it.
3. You had better fix it.   **You'd** better fix it.

Practice with Contractions: have*

1. I have been there.   **I've** been there.
2. I have already eaten   **I've** already eaten.
3. We have heard.   **We've** heard.
4. They have done it.   **They've** done it.
5. I would have done it.   I **would've** done it.
6. You should have told me.   You **should've** told me.
7. You must have seen it.   You **must've** seen it.

*Note: Americans generally contract the verb *have* only if it functions as an auxiliary verb. For example we say: "I've been" and "I've heard." But if *have* is the main verb, we don't say, "I've a car." We say, "I have a car."

Practice with Contractions: has

1. She has left.   **She's** left.
2. It has been fun.   **It's** been fun.
3. He has already eaten.   **He's** already eaten.
4. Who has seen the film?   **Who's** seen the film?

Practice with Contractions: is

Note that this contraction sounds the same as the contraction of *has*.

1. He is working.   **He's** working.
2. She is a teacher.   **She's** a teacher.
3. It is hot.   **It's** hot.
4. Sam is American.   **Sam's** American.
5. Mary is tall.   **Mary's** tall.
6. Dinner is ready.   **Dinner's** ready.

Practice with Contractions: am

1. I am fine.   **I'm** fine.
2. I am from Japan.   **I'm** from Japan.

Practice with Contractions: are

1. We are waiting.   **We're** waiting.
2. We are sorry.   **We're** sorry.
3. They are leaving.   **They're** leaving.
4. They are there.   **They're** there.
5. What are they doing?   **What're** they doing?
6. When are they coming? **When're** they coming?
7. Where are they going? **Where're** they going?

Practice with Contractions: not

1. I cannot swim.   I **can't** swim.
2. I should not go.   I **shouldn't** go.
3. I do not like it.   I **don't** like it.

Word Pairs for Practice
These words pairs are pronounced the same.

1. aisle	I'll	5. heel/heal	he'll
2. wheel	we'll	6. your	you're
3. there	they're	7. weave	we've
4. weed	we'd	8. heed	he'd

Practice with Contractions: Common Expressions

1. How's it going?
2. What's up?
3. What're you doing?
4. What've you been up to?
5. What's the matter?
6. What'll it be?
7. That'll be all.
8. It'll be hot.
9. It'll be good.
10. It'll rain.
11. How've you been?
12. Where're you going?
13. Where's he from?
14. Where're they from?
15. I'd like that.
16. Who's calling?
17. What's new?
18. I'm fine.

Practice Dialogues
Employee Meeting

a. Hi Tom. **I've** got a question. What **time's** our meeting?

b. **It'll** start at five.

a. Oh great. **I'm** glad **I'll** be able to make it. **Who's** coming?

b. **Let's** see… **Bob'll** be there,   **John'll** be there and **I'll** be there, but Mary **won't** make it. **She's** out of town.

a. How about Nick?

b. He **can't** make it. He said he **would've** come if **he'd** known about it earlier.

a. Is Vivian coming?

b. She said **she'd** like to make it, but **she's** got a lot of work to do.

a. **It'll** only last an hour, **won't** it?

b. Yes, **we'd** better keep it short. **Everybody'll** want to go home by six o'clock.

In the Restaurant

a. **I've** been looking forward to eating here.

b. Me too. **Everyone's** been talking about this place.

a. **What're** you gonna order?

b. **I'm** hungry. I think **I'd** like some meat tonight.

c. Hi folks. **I'll** be your waitress. Ready to order?

b. Yes, **we're** ready.

c. Great. **What'll** it be?

b. **She'll** have chicken and **I'll** have steak. And **we'll** both have a glass of red wine.

c. Is that it?

b. **That'll** be all.

c. Got it. Your **food'll** be ready in a few minutes.

Forgotten Birthday

a. It was my birthday two weeks ago.

b. Oh, I **must've** been too busy to look at my calendar. You **should've** told me. We **could've** celebrated together. I **would've** taken you out to dinner. Or I **could've** at least baked you a cake.

Song Lyrics for Practice
"After You've Gone"

After **you've** gone—and left me crying
After **you've** gone—**there's** no denying
You'll feel blue—**you're** gonna be sad
You've missed the dearest pal that you ever had

There'll come a time—**don't** forget it
There'll come a time—when **you'll** regret it

Some day when **you'll** grow lonely
Your heart will break like mine—**you'll** want me only

After **you've** gone—after **you've** gone away

(by Creamer/Layton)

Conditional Tense and Contractions

 CD 4 Track 49

The grammar of the conditional tense requires a lot of small words that you will need to learn to contract. For example, the following sentence which is the conditional past unreal tense contains thirteen short words: "If you had not called me I would not have known about it." Saying each word separately obviously sounds unnatural and very foreign. Here's how an American would say that: "If you hadn't called me, I wouldn've known about it." Instead of "wouldn't have," we say, "woudn've." The *t* of the word *not* disappears. Or, in more casual situations, the *have* of *would not have* sounds like *a* as in "woudna."

This grammar point is often difficult for some intermediate students of English. It might also be difficult for some advanced speakers who have learned English informally, just by speaking it in the United States, rather than through classroom study. Producing these conditional sentences quickly and naturally, particularly in the past unreal tense is difficult for many learners of English. If this is your case, make an extra effort to master this grammar point. Repeating the sentences of the following exercises will help you memorize the grammatical patterns. Practice them until you feel proficient using them.

Word Groups for Practice

 CD 4 Track 50

Let's start learning to use contractions in the easier part of the conditional past: the "*if* clause."

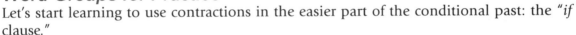

	sounds like:
1. If I had been...	"If I'd been..."
2. If I had not called...	"If I hadn't called..."
3. If she had seen...	"If she'd seen..."
4. If they had gone...	"If they'd gone..."

Now let's practice the second half of the past conditional sentence. There are two versions of this type of contraction: standard speech and casual speech.

	sounds like:	*casual speech:*
1. would have	"would've"	"woulda"
2. would not have	"wouldn've"	"wouldna"
3. could have	"could've"	"coulda"
4. could not have	"couldn've"	"couldna"
5. should not have	"shouldn've"	"shouldna"

Conditional Questions

With questions using *have* you must add an /ə/ sound between the pronoun and the contraction. But for statements, don't do this. For example a question like "Would you have been there?" would sound like "Would you'/ə/ve been there?" However, a statement would sound like: "You've been there."

	sounds like:
1. Would you have…?	"Would you'/ə/ve…?"
2. Would you have been…?	"Would you'/ə/ve been…?"
3. Would she have…?	"Would she'/ə/ve…. ?"
4. Would she have wanted…?	"Would she'/ə/ve wanted…?"

Practice Sentences

These sentences are all in the past conditional tense.

1. If **I'd** known it was your birthday, I **would've** gotten you a present.
2. If you **hadn't** been driving so fast, you **wouldn've** gotten a ticket.
3. If the **weather'd** been warmer, we **would've** gone to the park.
4. If **he'd** been more careful, he **wouldn've** had an accident.
5. I **would've** passed the test if **I'd** studied more.
6. Would **you'/ə/ve** done that, if **you'd** been in my shoes?
7. What would **you'/ə/ve** said if **she'd** asked you about it?
8. Where would **you'/ə/ve** gone if you **hadn't** come to the US?

Practice Sentences

The sentences below are examples of casual speech and use *a* instead of *'ve* for *have*

9. If it **hadn't** rained we **wouldna** canceled the picnic.
10. It **woulda** been more fun if **there'd** been more people at the party.
11. I **woulda** called you if **you'd** given me your number.
12. If **they'd** come on time, they **wouldna** missed their flight.
13. She **wouldna** known if you **hadn't** told her.

Practice Dialogue

a. What would you'/ə/ve done if you hadn't come to the United States?
b. If I hadn't come to the US, I would've lived with my family, and I wouldn've had to study English. I wouldn've met my wife. I would've married someone else.

Advice from a Successful Student

"Speak with confidence. I have learned that your insecurity will actually make your accent stronger. When I go on acting auditions, I first do my homework and work on my major mistakes, and then I let go of all that work and I just do it. I am just myself. So, if you have an important interview or speaking situation coming up, just relax and let your true self come out. Don't be inhibited."

Mauricio Sanchez, Actor, Venezuela

Casual Versus Formal Speech

Casual speech is used in an informal setting with friends and acquaintances. In casual situations, we are sometimes less careful with pronunciation and grammar. Remember, just like with contractions, there are rules to casual speech. Don't assume that you can randomly reduce any sounds that you feel like reducing. Doing this will only make your speech sound more foreign or more difficult to understand.

Casual speech has certain characteristics that distinguish it from formal speech. These are the main ones:

A. Sentences are shortened and grammar is simplified.

	sounds like:
1. Do you want to go?	"Wanna go?"
2. You'd better do it.	"You better do it."

B. Speakers are less careful about pronouncing every consonant.

	sounds like:
1. probably	"probly"
2. I don't know	"I dunno"
3. remember	"member"
4. going	"goin"
5. until	"til"
6. because	"cuz"

C. Slang is more acceptable.

	becomes:
1. I need five dollars.	"I need five bucks."
2. I don't have any money.	"I'm broke."

Below are some rules of the simplifications that are made in informal speech.

Rules and Patterns of Casual Speech		
Formal, Careful Speech	Informal, Relaxed Speech	Examples
you	ya	I'll call ya. See ya.
because	'cuz	I did it 'cuz I wanted to. I'm tired 'cuz I worked all day.
I don't know	I dunno	I dunno why. I dunno what to do.
let me	lemme	Lemme do it. Lemme help you. Lemme talk to him.
give me	gimme	Gimme a call. Gimme a break! Can you gimme a minute?
did you...?	joo	Joo call me? Why joo do it? Joo go out last night?
do you want to...?	wanna...?	Wanna go out? Wanna dance? What do you wanna do?
have got to...	gotta...	I gotta go. You gotta do it.
should've would've could've must've	shoulda woulda coulda musta	You shoulda told me. It woulda been nice. We coulda come. You musta seen it.
shouldn't have wouldn't have couldn't have	shouldna wouldna couldna	You shouldna done that. I woundna known. It couldna happened.
going to	gonna	I'm gonna go. It's gonna rain. What are you gonna do?
what do you...?	wadda you...?	Whadda you want? Whadda you doing? Whadda you think?

Rules and Patterns of Casual Speech		
Formal, Careful Speech	Informal, Relaxed Speech	Examples
a lot of	**a lotta**	That's a lotta money. I've got a lotta friends.
kind of	**kinda**	It's kinda hot. What kinda car is that?
out of	**adda**	Get adda here. I'm adda money. You're adda your mind. *meaning:* You're crazy.
go to	**goddu**	I go to work. Let's go to a concert.
yes	**yeah** **yup**	Yeah. It's good. Yup. I did it.
no	**nope**	Nope. I'm not going. Nope. That's not right.
-ing	**in'**	What are you doin'? Nothin' much.

Practice Dialogues

Invitation to a Movie

a. Whadda you doin' tonight?
b. I dunno yet. I think I'm gonna just stay home.
a. Wanna go to a movie?
b. I'm kinda tired. I gotta get up early tomorrow.
a. Joo go out last night?
b. Yeah, I shoudna gone to bed so late. I woulda had a lot more energy today.
a. Why don cha just take it easy then, and we'll go out some other time.
b. Okay, lemme know when you're free again. See ya.

Commonly Confused Words

The following pairs of words are often mispronounced and end up sounding the same when spoken by some non-native speakers.

	Pronunciation	Example
sell **sale**	*e* is /ɛ/ as in *get* *a* is /eɪ/ as in *take*	Would you like to **sell** it? Sorry, it's not for **sale**.
series **serious**	two syllables three syllables	I love that new TV **series**. Are you **serious**? I hate it.
color **collar**	*o* is /ə/ as in *fun* *o* is /ɑ/ as in *father*	Do you like the **color** of this shirt? Yes, but I want one with a **collar**.
costume **custom**	*o* is /ɑ/ as in *father* *u* is /ə/ as in *fun*	Children wear **costumes** for Halloween. Is that an American **custom**?
been **bean**	ee is /I/ as in *sit* ee is /i/ as in *meet*	What have you **been** cooking? I've been cooking **beans**.
of **off**	*f* is a /v/ sound *o* is /ɑ/ as in *father*	What are you thinking **of**? I'm thinking of taking the day **off**.
want **won't**	*a* is /ɑ/ as in *father* *o* is /ou/ as in *boat*	Do you **want** to go? No, I **won't** go.
dessert **desert**	second syllable stress first syllable stress	I had **dessert** after dinner. They drove through the **desert**.
where **were**	*er* is/ɛər/ as in *care* *er* is /ər/ as in *bird*	**Where** did they go? They **were** here a minute ago.
wonder **wander**	*o* is /ə/ as in *fun* *a* is /ɑ/ as in *father*	I **wonder** where they are. They're probably **wandering** in the forest.
warm **worm**	*or* is /ɔr/ as in *for* *or* is /ɚ/ as in *bird*	It's a **warm** day. There's a **worm** in my apple.
woman **women**	*o* is /ʊ/ as in *good* *o* is /I/ as in *sit*	She is a nice **woman**. All of the **women** here are nice.
potty **party**	*t* is almost /d/ sounds like "pardy" ("fast d" sound)	The little boy wants to go **potty**. He's at the birthday **party**.

Chapter Nine

MEMORIZING THE EXCEPTIONS

This chapter consists of words that are commonly mispronounced by non-native speakers. Some of these pairs of words are spelled the same but pronounced differently. Others are spelled differently but pronounced the same. Sometimes the same word exists in other languages but it has a different pronunciation. There is also a list of the most common words with silent consonants and another one with disappearing syllables. Finally, there is list of words that are universally hard to pronounce, even by some native speakers. But the goal of an educated speaker of English is to always use language well and to pronounce words clearly and correctly.

As you will see in this chapter, English is full of illogical spelling rules and exceptions. Fortunately, if you make it a point to memorize the correct pronunciation of the commonly used words that are in this chapter, you will certainly feel more confident about your accent.

Same Spelling, Different Pronunciation

Below are common words that are spelled the same but have different pronunciations and different meanings.

	Pronunciation	Meaning
bass **bass**	*a* is /ae/ as in *fat* *a* is /eɪ/ as in *take*	a kind of fish a musical instrument, or low voice or tone
desert **desert**	first syllable stress second syllable stress	dry land with little or no vegetation to leave empty or alone, to abandon
dove **dove**	*o* is /ə/ as in *fun* *o* is /ou/ as in *boat*	a kind of bird similar to a pigeon past tense of *dive*
lead **lead**	*ea* is /i/ as in *meet* *ea* is /ɛ/ as in *get*	to guide a kind of metal
minute **minute**	*i* is /I/ as in *sit* (first syllable stress) *i* is /aɪ/ as in *time* (second syllable stress)	sixty seconds very small, tiny
Polish **polish**	*o* is /ou/ as in *boat* *o* is /ɑ/ as in *father*	(adjective) from Poland to make a surface shine

	Pronunciation	Meaning
refuse **refuse**	second syllable stress first syllable stress	(verb) to deny, reject (noun) trash, garbage
resume **resume**	final *e* is silent (second syllable stress) final *e* is /eɪ/ as in *take* (first syllable stress)	to begin again after an interruption a summary of work experience
tear **tear**	rhymes with *care* rhymes with *here*	to separate by force a drop of liquid coming from the eye
wind **wind**	*i* is /I/ as in *sit* *i* is /aɪ/ as in *time*	outdoor current of air to turn in circular motions
wound **wound**	*ou* is /u/ as in *food* *ou* is /aʊ/ as in *house*	injury, especially when skin is torn or cut past tense of verb *wind*

Two Correct Pronunciations

There are two ways of pronouncing the following words. Both choices are acceptable.

1. either	*ei* is /i/ as in *meet* *ei* is /aɪ/ as in *time*	(more common in American English) (British English)
2. neither	*ei* is /i/ as in *meet* *ei* is /aɪ/ as in *time*	(more common in American English) (British English)
3. data	*a* is /eɪ/ as in *take* *a* is /æ/ as in *fat*	(more common) (less common)
4. aunt	*a* is /æ/ as in *fat* *a* is /ɑ/ as in *father*	(more common) (less common)
5. apricot	*a* is /eɪ/ as in *take* *a* is /æ/ as in *fat*	(more common) (less common)

Especially Difficult Words

The following words are frequently mispronounced by non-native speakers either because a similar sounding word exists in other languages, or because the spelling is unusual. Other times the combination of sounds simply makes the words difficult to say—even for native speakers!

Difficult Word	Correct Pronunciation	Incorrect Pronunciation	Example
1. aluminum	four syllables	In many languages, and in British English, this word has five syllables and is spelled *aluminium*	I will wrap my leftover food in **aluminum** foil.
2. caffeine	two syllables /kæf-in/	three syllables /kæf-ɛ-in/	I had too much **caffeine** and couldn't fall asleep.
3. chaos	/keɪ - ɑs/	"house"	The apartment was in complete **chaos** after the burglary.
4. choir	sounds like: "k+wire"	"core"	The children's **choir** sang at the church.
5. cooperate	four syllables *oo*= two separate sounds that sound like "kou – ap"	three syllables	Children, please **cooperate** with your teacher.
6. cucumber	first *u* sounds like *you*	first *u* sounds like /u/	I made a tomato and **cucumber** salad.
7. entrepreneur	fourth syllable stress first *e* sounds like /ə/	first *e* sounds like /ɛ/	That business was bought by a foreign **entrepreneur**.
8. Europe	first syllable stress, *o* is reduced /ə/ sound	second syllable stress	Many languages are spoken in **Europe**.
9. foreigner	first syllable stress *eign* sounds like *en* *ig* are silent letters	second syllable stress	I don't want to speak English like a **foreigner**.
10. hierarchy	first syllable stress *heir* sounds like "hire"	second syllable stress	Honesty is the first of my **heirarchy** of values.

Difficult Word	Correct Pronunciation	Incorrect Pronunciation	Example
11. hygiene	two syllables: sounds like "hi + jean"	three syllables	In the medical environment **hygiene** is very important.
12. jewelry	*l* and *r* together "jewel+ ree"	vowel separating *l* and *r* "joo – le – ry"	I bought a gold necklace at the **jewelry** store.
13. length	pronounce *g*	silent *g*	What is the **length** of that swimming pool?
14. museum	say: m + *you* + *zee* + /əm/ stress second syllable	"moo" +"zei" + "oom"	Let's see the new art exhibit at the **museum**.
15. of	*f* sounds like *v* *o* is reduced /ə/ sound	"off"	What is it made **of**?
16. parentheses	second syllable stress	third syllable stress	Please write the information in **parentheses**.
17. pizza	sounds like "peet+sa"	"pee+za"	We were hungry so we ordered a large **pizza**.
18. protein	two syllables "pro + teen"	three syllables "pro-te-een"	Meat and eggs contain a lot of **protein**.
19. recipe	three syllables; final *e* sounds like "ee"	two syllables silent *e*	Can you give me the **recipe** for this delicious cheesecake?
20. schedule	*sch* sounds like "sk" *du* sounds like "ju"	*sch* = "sh"	I don't like my new work **schedule**.
21. schizophrenia	*sch* sounds like "sk"	*sch* = "sh"	The psychiatrist was working with patients who have **schizophrenia**.
22. science	two syllables sci + /y/tence	one syllable "signs"	I got a good grade in my **science** class.
23. strength	pronounce "*g*"	silent "*g*"	I don't have enough **strength** to carry that.
24. thermometer	second syllable stress	third syllable stress	I will check my fever with a **thermometer**.

Practice Sentences

1. I placed the frozen **pizza** on the **aluminum** foil.
2. I found a **recipe** for a **cucumber** salad.
3. Too much **caffeine** makes me feel **schizophrenic**.
4. We can **cooperate** and create a **hierarchy**.
5. That **foreigner** is an **entrepreneur** from **Europe**.
6. The **schedule** of the **choir** rehearsal is in **parentheses**.
7. They need better **hygiene** and less **chaos**.
8. The **thermometer** is used in the **science** class.

Words with Dropped Syllables

When pronouncing the following list of words, do not pronounce all of the syllables. Instead of saying "choc-o-late," with three syllables, say "choc-late" with only two syllables. Instead of "brocc-o-li," say "brocc-li." In both of those words one of the middle vowels disappears. Below is a list of the most common words that have a dropped syllable.

1. actually	9. every	17. favorite	25. desperate
2. aspirin	10. family	18. interest	26. diamond
3. average	11. generally	19. interesting	27. diaper
4. basically	12. broccoli	20. laboratory	28. practically
5. beverage	13. business	21. liberal	29. preference
6. different	14. camera	22. opera	30. several
7. extraordinary	15. catholic	23. comfortable	31. temperature
8. evening	16. chocolate	24. coverage	32. theory

Practice Dialogues

1. a. What's your **favorite vegetable**?
   b. I like **broccoli**.

2. a. Is he **Catholic**?
   b. Yes, he comes from a **Catholic family**.

3. a. Do you like my **diamond** ring?
   b. It's really **extraordinary**.

4. a. Would you like some **chocolate**?
   b. Yes, I'll take **several** pieces.

5. a. What are you doing this **evening**?
   b. I'm going to the **opera**.

6. a. Is the **temperature** okay for you?
   b. Yes, it's quite **comfortable** here.

7. a. Do you need some **aspirin**?
   b. Yes, **desperately**.

8. a. Do you agree with that **theory**?
   b. I think it's an **interesting theory**.

9. a. Do you like that **restaurant**?
   b. Yes, they have many **different beverages**.

10. a. What is your **preference**?
    b. **Actually**, I don't have a **preference**. I'm **indifferent**.

Words with Silent Letters

The chart below highlights many common words that have a letter that is not pronounced.

silent *b*	bomb, debt, limb, thumb, crumb, doubt, numb, tomb, climb, dumb, plumber, comb, lamb, subtle
silent *c*	indict, muscle
silent *ch*	yacht
silent *d*	adjective, adjust, handsome, Wednesday
silent *g*	align, campaign, diaphragm, resign, assign, champagne, foreign, sign, benign, design, reign
silent *gh*	bright, fight, light, bought, fought, night, caught, height, weigh, drought, high, weight
silent *h*	ghost, heir, honest, hour, honor, herb, vehicle, exhibit
silent *k*	knee, knife, know, knot
silent *l*	calm, folk, psalm, talk, chalk, half, salmon, walk, could, Lincoln, should, would
silent *n*	hymn, autumn, column
silent *p*	cupboard, pneumonia, psalm, psychology, psychic, receipt
silent *s*	aisle, debris, island, Arkansas, Illinois
silent *t*	ballet, Chevrolet, mortgage, gourmet, bouquet, Christmas, often, debut, buffet, fasten, whistle, soften, castle, listen, fillet, rapport
silent *th*	asthma, months,* clothes*
silent *w*	answer, sword, toward

*You will hear some Americans lightly pronounce the *th* sound when saying these words but most just omit it.

Homophones

Homophones are words with the same pronunciation but different spelling and meaning. Make sure you pronounce the second (and sometimes third) word the same as the first word, even though they look different.

1. Adam–atom	32. flea–flee	63. profit–prophet
2. air–err–heir	33. flew–flu	64. rain–rein–reign
3. aloud–allowed	34. flower–flour	65. red–read
4. altar–alter	35. for–four	66. right–write
5. ant–aunt	36. Greece–grease	67. ring–wring
6. ate–eight	37. guest–guessed	68. road–rode–rowed
7. band–banned	38. gym–Jim	69. roll–role
8. bare–bear	39. heal–heel–he'll	70. root–route
9. base–bass	40. hear–here	71. sail–sale
10. be–bee	41. him–hymn	72. sea–see
11. beat–beet	42. hire–higher	73. seam–seem
12. berry–bury	43. hole–whole	74. seas–sees–seize
13. billed–build	44. I–eye	75. seen–scene
14. blew–blue	45. I'll–isle–aisle	76. seller–cellar
15. board–bored	46. in–inn	77. side–sighed
16. brake–break	47. lessen–lesson	78. so–sow–sew
17. buy–by–bye	48. maid –made	79. some–sum
18. caller–collar	49. mail–male	80. son–sun
19. cell–sell	50. meat–meet	81. steal–steel
20. cent–sent–scent	51. metal–medal	82. sweet–suite
21. chili–chilly–Chile	52. new–knew	83. tail–tale
22. chews–choose	53. nose–knows	84. there–their–they're
23. cite–site –sight	54. not–knot	85. tie–Thai
24. close–clothes	55. nun–none	86. to–too–two
25. core–corps	56. oh–owe	87. tow–toe
26. course–coarse	57. one–won	88. weather–whether
27. dear–deer	58. our–hour	89. wheel–we'll
28. die–dye	59. pail–pale	90. wore–war
29. do–due–dew	60. pair–pare	91. worn–warn
30. finish–Finnish	61. past–passed	
31. feudal–futile	62. peace–piece	

Practice Sentences

The highlighted words are homophones, so they pronounce them the same.

1. If they **hire** him, he'll have a **higher** salary.
2. Reading **aloud** is not **allowed** in the library.
3. I **passed** by your house in the **past**.
4. I **hear** that he's been **here**.
5. I **rode** my bike on the **road**.
6. Her young **son** went out in the **sun**.

7. He **knows** about your broken **nose**.

8. Only **one** team **won**.

9. I **read** the **red** book.

10. I have a **male mail** carrier.

Practice Dialogues

1. a. Does the **nun** have children?
   b. No, she has **none**.

2. a. Have you **seen** it?
   b. I have never **seen** such a strange **scene**.

3. a. When did the soldier wear the uniform?
   b. He **wore** it in the **war**.

4. a. I want **two**, and you?
   b. I want **two**, **too**.

5. a. Are they **there** already?
   b. **They're** already **there**.
   a. Where?
   b. At **their** uncle's house.

6. a. You should **dye** your hair green.
   b. I'd rather **die** than **dye** it green.

7. a. Is the gold **medal** really made of gold?
   b. I think the **medal** is made of **metal**.

8. a. Did I **write** that correctly?
   b. Yes, that's **right**.

9. a. What time did you eat?
   b. I **ate** at **eight**.

10. a. How's the weather in **Chile**.
    b. Sometimes it's **chilly** in **Chile**.

11. a. **Do** you know when the report is **due**?
    b. Yes, I **do**. It's **due** on Tuesday.

12. a. He broke his foot and injured his **heel**.
    b. I hope that **he'll heal** soon.

13. a. I **owe** ten thousand dollars.
    b. **Oh**, you **owe** so much.

14. a. Do you want to **sail** the boat today?
    b. I can't. My favorite store has a big **sale**.

NATIVE LANGUAGE GUIDE

This language guide will give you an overview of the sections of this book that you especially need to work on. This does not mean that you should neglect the rest of the book. All non-native speakers need to learn about syllable stress, word stress, and intonation which create the pattern of natural sounding American speech. These topics are covered in Chapters Five through Seven. Also, Chapter Eight, "Sounds Like a True Native Speaker," and Chapter Nine, "Memorizing the Exceptions," are very important for all foreign speakers of English to master.

For a detailed analysis of your accent (which will help you to use this book more efficiently) or for accent reduction training you may contact *masteringtheamericanaccent.com* or call 1-800 - 871-1317.

Chinese

Consonants

The /n/ sound
This consonant sound is one of the biggest problems for Chinese speakers, who tend to either completely drop the /n/ or pronounce it incorrectly when it is at the **end of the word** as in "pho<u>n</u>e" or **before another consonant** as in "no<u>n</u>se<u>n</u>se."

Linking the final /n/ of a word to the vowel of the next word automatically solves this problem. So, when "can eat" becomes "c/æ/ + neat," the problem is solved. You should always practice linking words since this will fix other consonant problems that occur at the end of the word, particularly with the letters *m*, *r*, *d*, *t*, and *th*.

If there is not a vowel sound following the difficult consonant, it's a bit more challenging. You will need to really make an extra effort to clearly pronounce this sound and other consonant sounds that never occur at the ends of Chinese words.

The /n/ sound is never a problem when it is in the beginning of the word because the Chinese *n* in this position is the same as the American *n*. The American *n* sound is always produced in the front of the mouth, with the tip of the tongue touching the gum ridge which is behind the upper teeth. The Chinese /n/ sound is produced in the back of the mouth, with the back of the tongue touching the upper part of the mouth, similar to the "ng" sound in English. This is why some Chinese speakers of English tend to pronounce *thin* and *thing* the same way.

Practice Words

When the tip of your tongue makes contact with the gum ridge, make sure that you are continuing to produce sound by allowing air to come out through your nose. Otherwise your *n* will be silent, and will not sound like the American /n/.

1. one	4. man	7. nine	10. nineteen
2. invent	5. convent	8. pronounce	11. content
3. financial	6. attention	9. mention	12. consonant

Practice Sentences

1. He came to London in nineteen ninety nine.
2. He gained ten pounds in one month.
3. The sun shone after the rain.
4. That town is known for its fine wine.

The /l/ sound

All explanations and exercises for this /l/ sound are in Chapter Four. Make sure you learn to correctly produce a strong American *l*. Otherwise you will end up pronouncing *code* and *cold*, and *too* and *tool*, the same.

As you are raising the tongue for the /l/, don't raise the jaw with it. Look in the mirror and try to make your tongue move up without the jaw moving. This will strengthen your tongue and help you to create a better sounding *l*.

Confusing /n/ and /l/

Make sure you do not confuse *n* and *l*, especially with words that contain both of these sounds, as in *analysis* or *only*. The primary difference between the two sounds is the location of the air flow. For *n* the air is coming out through your nose, whereas for *l* the air is coming out through the sides of your mouth. The tongue position is very similar for these two sounds. The tip of the tongue is a bit flatter for the *n*. With the *l* the jaw needs to open more to create space for the air to come out through the sides of the mouth. Practice keeping the jaw open while only moving the tongue for the *l*.

The /r/ Sound

All explanations and exercises for pronouncing *r* are in Chapter Four. Make sure that you clearly pronounce the final *r* at the end of words and before another consonant.

common mistake:	*should be:*
1. "mo"	"mo<u>r</u>e"
2. "foam"	"fo<u>r</u>m"
3. "moaning"	"mo<u>r</u>ning"
4. "pot"	"pa<u>r</u>t"
5. "fa"	"fa<u>r</u>"
6. "cone"	"co<u>r</u>n"
7. "tone"	"torn"
8. "motha"	"mothe<u>r</u>"
9. "ha"	"he<u>r</u>"

The /v/ Sound

Native Chinese speakers have a tendency to drop /v/ in the middle or at the end of words. If you are speaking quickly, make sure that you don't drop the *v*. All explanations and exercises for this sound are in Chapter Four.

common mistake:	*should be:*
"fai dollars"	"fi<u>v</u>e dollars"
"goment"	"go<u>v</u>ernment"
"involed"	"invol<u>v</u>ed"

Practice Sentences

1. I ha<u>v</u>e to ha<u>v</u>e fi<u>v</u>e.
2. He will pro<u>v</u>e that he can impro<u>v</u>e the go<u>v</u>ernment.
3. I ha<u>v</u>e been invol<u>v</u>ed with them for ele<u>v</u>en or twel<u>v</u>e years.

Also pay close attention to words with *w*. Do not make the common mistake of confusing the /v/ and /w/ sounds. All explanations and exercises for /v/ versus /w/ sounds are also in Chapter Four.

typical mistake:	*should be:*
"ha<u>we</u>"	"ha<u>v</u>e"

The /z/ Sound

Sometimes Chinese speakers skip the /z/ sound. Make sure you have a strong /z/ sound in the middle and end of words. note that this sound is often spelled with an *s*. Also, be careful when there is a *th* and an *s* in the same word or near each other.

1. po<u>s</u>ition   3. becau<u>se</u>   5. thou<u>s</u>and
2. bu<u>s</u>iness   4. ea<u>sy</u>   6. the<u>se</u>

Consonant Clusters

Consonant clusters (two or more consonants together) don't occur in Chinese words, so there's a tendency for Chinese speakers to pronounce only the first consonant of the group. Therefore *card* can sound like "car" and *extra* can sound like "estra." Remember, the letter *x* represents two sounds: /ks/. When there are two or more consonants next to each other, make sure that you pronounce *every* consonant. Review the "consonant clusters" section in Chapter Four for more information.

one consonant:	*two consonants:*
Where's your car?	Where's your car**d**?
They ask about it.	They ask**ed** about it.

Vowels

It is recommended that you study all of the American vowel sounds in detail. (See Chapters One and Two.) However, pay special attention to the vowel sounds highlighted below which are the most problematic ones for Chinese speakers of English.

The /eɪ/ sound

For native Chinese speakers the /eɪ/ sound creates by far the biggest vowel error when it is followed by *n*, *m*, or *l*. The formation of these consonants sometimes prevents the tongue from moving correctly for the /eɪ/ sound. Generally this /eɪ/ tends to be pronounced as /ɛ/ or /æ/ making the pronunciation of *pain*, *pen*, and *pan* sound similar or the same when Chinese speakers pronounce them. Also, *sale* and *sell* will often sound the same. Here's a technique for fixing this problem.

Chances are you say *rain* and *ran* similarly or the same. To fix this problem say the word *ray*, then slowly add the /n/ sound. Seeing them as separate in your mind will help you to fully pronounce both of the vowel sounds before you begin to move your tongue into the *n* position.

The /eɪ/ sound is easier for Chinese speakers to produce if it is at the end of the word or when it is followed by any other consonant. It's generally only a problem when it's followed by an *n*, *m*, or *l*.

Words for Practice

Let's practice the technique described above by saying some common words that have /eɪ/ + /n/, /m/, or /l/. First say the word that ends in /eɪ/ and then slowly add the consonant sound.

/eɪ/	/eɪ/ + /n/	/eɪ/ + /l/	/eɪ/ + /m/
may	may + /n/ = "main"	may + /l/ = "male"	
say	say + /n/ = "sane"	say + /l/ = "sale"	say + /m/ = "same"
way	way + /n/ = "Wayne"	way + /l/ = "whale"	
stay	stay + /n/ = "stain"	stay + /l/ = "stale"	
gay	gay + /n/ = "gain"	gay + /l/ = "Gail"	gay + /m/ = "game"
pay	pay + /n/ = "pain"	pay + /l/ = "pail"	pay + /m/ = "payment"

Words Contrasts for Practice
Make sure you pronounce the two words in each pair below differently.

	/ɛ/	/eɪ/		/ɛ/	/eɪ/
1.	sell	sale	4.	men	main
2.	well	whale	5.	pen	pain
3.	tell	tale	6.	plan	plain

Confusing /ɛ/ and /æ/
Confusing these two vowel sounds will cause you to pronounce *men* and *man* the same way. Review Chapters One and Two to fix this type of error.

Confusing /i/ and /eɪ/
Make sure you pronounce these vowel sounds differently. Pay special attention to words that end with the /i/ sound: *very, actually, really, me,* and *we.* Make sure the /i/ is long.

Word Contrasts for Practice

	/eɪ/	/i/		/eɪ/	/i/
1.	way	we	6.	hay	he
2.	say	see	7.	may	me
3.	slave	sleeve	8.	fail	feel
4.	grain	green	9.	raid	reed
5.	straight	street			

Sentence Pairs for Practice

/eɪ/	/i/
1. What did you **say**?	What did you **see**?
2. They **ate** pork.	They **eat** pork.
3. I had the **mail**.	I had the **meal**.
4. When did you **fail** it?	When did you **feel** it?

Longer Words

Since all Chinese words consist of only one syllable, there is a tendency for speakers of Mandarin and Cantonese to reduce English words with longer syllables. Make sure you pronounce every syllable of longer words. Also, pronounce *every* consonant and don't lose vocal energy toward the end of the word. Pay special attention to this if you tend to speak fast. Don't take any short cuts! Below are some examples of English words typically cut short by native Chinese speakers.

		typical mistake (missing syllable)	should be pronounced:	correct number of syllables
1.	particularly	"par-ti-cu-ly"	"par-tic-u-lar-ly"	5
2.	government	"gov-ment"	"gov-ern-ment"	3
3.	visual	"vis-ul"	"vi-su-al"	3
4.	usual	"us-al"	"u -su - al"	3
5.	experience	"exper-ince"	"ek-spe-ri-ence"	4
6.	immediately	"im-me-di-ly"	"im-me-di-at-ely"	5
7.	customer	"cus-mer"	"cus-tom-er"	3

Practice Sentences

The correct number of syllables is indicated above each word. Count them as you read the words, then try to say them more quickly making sure you are not skipping any syllable.

1. The scientist is enthusiastic about artificial intelligence.
    (3)   (5)   (4)   (4)

2. I am confident that this advertisement will be meaningful to the customers.
         (3)   (4)   (3)   (3)

3. It is unimaginable that the Europeans lost the championship.
        (6)   (4)   (4)

4. The foreigner had a powerful vocabulary and communicated confidently.
       (3)   (3)   (5)   (5)   (4)

5. The executive assistant primarily negotiated for the president.
       (4)   (3)   (4)   (5)   (3)

6. We are investigating the developmental processes of our biggest competitors.
         (5)   (5)   (3)   (2)   (4)

7. I primarily practice the pronunciation of the difficult sentences.
     (4)   (5)   (3)   (3)

8. The entertainment industry is concentrated in Hollywood.
       (4)   (3)   (4)   (3)

9. He is seriously investigating a career in technical consulting.
        (4)   (5)   (3)   (3)

10. There is a spectacular exhibition at the museum.
                   (4)   (4)   (3)

Word Ending Errors

The endings of words can sometimes cause problems for the native Chinese speaker. For example, since **plural forms** don't exist in Chinese, there is a tendency to omit them when speaking English.

typical mistake:
"I have many American friend."

should be:
"I have many American friend**s**."

Another difficulty sometimes arises with the third person singular. The form of the verb doesn't change in Chinese so you may tend to omit the final *s*.

typical mistake:
"My friend say hello"

should be:
"My friend say**s** hello"

Finally, many native speakers of Chinese, even those who are very proficient in English, tend to randomly interchange the **present and past tenses.** Since these tense differences don't exist in Chinese it is understandably confusing.

typical mistake:
"I work yesterday."
"I usually forgot."

should be:
"I work**ed** yesterday."
"I usually forget."

Linking

Chinese speakers of English tend to pronounce each word separately, which makes the section on linking in Chapter Eight one of the most important aids in helping you sound more American. You will definitely want to review that chapter, but to summarize: **don't release the final consonant if it's "a stop."**

typical mistake:	*should be:*
"I had /ə/ lunch." or "I hada lunch."	"I had lunch."
"I used /ə/ to..." or "I useda to..."	"I used to..."
"I made /ə/ that." or "I made a that."	"I made that."

This mistake can be prevented by holding the final consonant and immediately saying the next word with no air created between pronouncing the two words. Study the section related to linking consonant + consonant in Chapter 8 for more practice.

Farsi

Study the whole book, but also pay special attention to a few points directly related to native Farsi speakers. These are outlined below.

Consonants

The *th* Sound

Review Chapters Three and Four to learn the correct pronunciation of this sound. Note that you might make the common mistake of substituting a /t/ or a /d/ for a *th*.

typical mistake:	*should be:*
"tank"	"<u>th</u>ank"
"dose"	"<u>th</u>ose"
"mudder"	"mo<u>th</u>er"

Confusing /v/ and /w/

All explanations and exercises for the "v" and "w" sounds are in Chapter Four. Be careful not to make the common mistake below.

typical mistake:	*should be:*
"<u>v</u>ine"	"<u>w</u>ine"
"very <u>v</u>ell"	"very <u>w</u>ell"

The /s/ Sound + Consonant

The Farsi language has no word that begins with an *s* and is followed by another consonant. There is usually a vowel in front of the *s*. Therefore, you will have a tendency to put an extra /ə / sound before English words that begin with this letter. Make sure you don't insert an extra vowel sound when you say the following words:

typical mistake:	*should be:*
"<u>es</u>mart"	"<u>sm</u>art"
"<u>es</u>tate"	"<u>st</u>ate"
"I am going to /ə/<u>sch</u>ool."	"I am going to <u>sch</u>ool."
"I /ə/<u>st</u>udy /ə/<u>Sp</u>anish."	"I study <u>Sp</u>anish."

The /l/ sound

Make sure that you don't quickly release the tip of your tongue for the *l* at the ends of words. This will cause you to over-pronounce the /l/. The American /l/ sound is softer and longer than the Farsi /l/, and the tip of the tongue is more relaxed. Review the exercises for the American /l/ sound in Chapter Four.

Pronouncing *ing*

Over-pronouncing *ing* is another common mistake for Farsi speakers. Make sure you don't release the /g/ sound in words that end with *ing*, such as *going* and *doing*. Review the rules for this sound in Chapter Four.

The /r/ Sound

You need to learn to create the correct American /r/ sound by studying Chapter Three, and doing all of the /r/ exercises in Chapter Four. Make sure you do not roll the /r/ with the tip of your tongue, as this creates a harsh-sounding Farsi /r/.

Farsi speakers tend to roll the /r/ particularly when it is followed by another consonant (as in b_ring, p_rogram, f_riend) or when it is in the beginning of a word (such as _red and _right).

Vowels

It is recommended that you study all of the American vowel sounds in detail. (See Chapters One and Two.) However, pay special attention to the vowel sounds highlighted below which are the most problematic ones for Iranian speakers of English.

The /I/ Sound

You might have a tendency to pronounce /I/ (as in sit) incorrectly. Make sure you pronounce the following words differently:

/I/	/i/
1. sit	seat
2. live	leave
3. fill	feel

The /ə/ Sound

You might confuse /ə/ as in *fun*, with /ɑ/ as in *hop*. Practice pronouncing the following words differently:

/ɑ/	/ə/
1. shot	shut
2. lock	luck
3. cop	cup

The /ʊ/ Sound

Do not make the common error of confusing /ʊ/ as in *good*, with /u/ as in *food*. Make sure that you pronounce the following words differently:

/ʊ/	/u/
1. full	fool
2. pull	pool
3. look	Luke

Syllable Stress

Speakers of Farsi tend to stress the first syllables of English words. Since there are a lot of exceptions to the rules of English syllable stress, you will need to simply memorize the words that you commonly use.

common mistake:	*should be:*
however	how**ever**
I'm from **I**ran.	I'm from Ir**an**.
Good **after**noon.	Good after**noon**.

Intonation

There's a tendency for Farsi speakers to use rising intonation. This can unintentionally create a tone that sounds sarcastic or doubtful. Study the rules of falling intonation in Chapter Seven. Don't overly prolong the final part of words and sentences and try not to go up in pitch, unless you're asking a "yes/no question."

Filipino Languages

Study the whole book, but also pay special attention to the topics outlined below which are the common trouble areas for Filipino speakers of English.

Consonants

Confusing /p/ and /f/

People from the Philippines substitute a /p/ for an /f/ sound. This type of mistake is parallel to the also common /v/ and /b/ confusion, and it requires you to focus on using either two lips or just the lower lip. Be particularly careful with words that contain both a *p* and an *f* or when these two sounds are close together as in: *perfect, perform, puffy, helpful, full page,* and *cup of coffee.*

The /*th*/ Sound

Review Chapters Three and Four to learn the correct pronunciation of this sound. A common mistake for native Tagalog speakers is to substitute a /t/ or a /d/ for the *th*.

typical mistake:	*should be:*
"tank"	"**th**ank"
"dose"	"**th**ose"
"mudder"	"mo**th**er"

Confusing /b/ and /v/

Practice the exercises in Chapter Four. Remember, the /b/ sound requires the lips to be completely closed, with no air coming out, whereas the /v/ sound only involves the lower lip, which touches the upper teeth and creates a vibrating air flow. Be particularly careful with words that contain both a *b* and *v* or when these sounds are close together as in: *Beverly, November, vibrate, available, I've been* and *very big.*

Confusing /s/ and /z/

The *s* in many English words is frequently pronounced as a /z/ sound. Learn the rules for this pronunciation and refer to the list in Chapter Four, common /z/-sound words. Words pronounced with a /z/ sound include: *husband, design, observe, always, and chose.*

Words Pairs for Practice

Make sure you say these pairs of words differently:

	/s/	/z/
1.	piece	peas
2.	face	phase
3.	bus	buzz
4.	price	prize

Confusing *sh* and *ch*
Make sure you can pronounce <u>*ch*</u>ose and <u>*sh*</u>oes differently. If you feel you need more practice, review these sounds in detail in Chapter Four.

Consonant Clusters
When a word contains two consonants next to each other, make sure that you pronounce both consonants. Review the last section of Chapter Four for further practice.

Words for Practice
Practice the following words with consonant clusters:

1. ju<u>st</u>
2. a<u>ct</u>
3. lo<u>st</u>
4. ha<u>nd</u>
5. pai<u>nt</u>
6. proje<u>ct</u>
7. mi<u>xed</u>
8. pai<u>nt</u>
9. se<u>nse</u>
10. de<u>sks</u>

Vowels

It is recommended that you study all of the American vowel sounds in detail. (See Chapters One and Two.) However, pay special attention to the vowel sounds highlighted below which are the most problematic ones for Filipino speakers of English.

Words Spelled with *o*
English words spelled with *o* are particularly difficult since *o* is usually pronounced as /ɑ/ as in *stop* and *hot*, but it can also be pronounced as /ə/ as in *love* and *Monday* or even as /ou/ as in *so* and *only*.

The /I/ Sound
Pay attention to this tricky short vowel. Make sure you pronounce the words in each pair below differently:

/I/	/i/
1. sit	seat
2. live	leave
3. fill	feel

The /ə/ Sound
Practice pronouncing the following words differently:

/ɑ/	/ə/
1. shot	shut
2. lock	luck
3. cop	cup

The /ʊ/ Sound

The /ʊ/ sound, as in *good*, can also pose problems for you. Make sure you pronounce the words in each pair below differently:

	/ʊ/	/u/
1.	full	fool
2.	pull	pool
3.	look	Luke

Word Stress

Filipino speakers stress the adjective more than the noun in their native language. In English, the noun is stressed more than the adjective.

typical mistake:

"That's a **nice** car."

"He's an **intelligent** man."

should be:

"That's a nice **car**."

"He's an intelligent **man.**"

Similarly, Filipinos tend to stress the first content word of a phrase or a sentence, whereas in English the last content word gets the most stress.

typical mistake:

"I **drove** my car."

"I **went** to the bank."

should be:

"I drove my **car**."

"I went to the **bank**."

Other common word stress errors:

typical mistake:

"I **should** go."

"**Turn** it off."

"**U**CLA"

should be:

"I should **go**."

"Turn it **off**."

"UC**LA**"

Study all of the other rules of word stress in Chapters Five through Eight and practice the exercises over and over.

French

Study the whole book, but also pay special attention to the topics outlined below. These are the common areas of difficulty for native French speakers.

Consonants

The Letter *h*

Make sure you pronounce the *h* sound at the beginning of words. The *h* is always pronounced in English except in these common words: *hour, honest, honor, herb, heir, exhaust, vehicle,* and *ghost.*

common mistake:	*should be:*
"she as"	"she <u>h</u>as"
"uman"	" <u>h</u>uman"

Word Contrasts for Practice

Make sure you pronounce the words in each pair differently:

no /h/	/h/
1. art	heart
2. air	hair
3. ate	hate
4. angry	hungry

Native French speakers also have a tendency to insert an /h/ sound where there shouldn't be one.

common mistake:	*should be:*
"he *h*is"	"he is"
"he's *h*at home"	"he's at home"
"*h*i hate"	"I hate"

Practice Sentences

1. Henry hardly ever has a headache.
2. Perhaps he hasn't heard of the hypothesis.
3. Have you ever eaten homemade Hungarian food?
4. I hope his habit doesn't make him an alcoholic.
5. The horror movie had a horrible ending.

The Final *s*

In French, the *s* at the end of words is almost always silent. Make sure that you clearly pronounce all of the *s* endings when speaking English.

common mistake:	*should be:*
"one of my uncle"	"one of my uncle<u>s</u>"
"a few problem"	"a few problem<u>s</u>"

Confusing *th* with /s/ or /z/

Review the exercises for these sounds in Chapter Four. Be especially careful with words that have a *th* and *s* sound near each other, such as <u>*thousand*</u> and <u>*south*</u>.

Word Contrasts for Practice

Make sure you don't pronounce these pairs of words the same:

s	*th*
1. mass	math
2. pass	path
3. seem	theme
4. all so	although

The /r/ Sound

When it appears at the end of a word or before another consonant, the /r/ sound may pose some difficulties for the native French speaker. Review the explanations and exercises for the /r/ sound in Chapter Four. Make sure you pronounce the final /r/ at the end of words.

typical mistake:	*should be:*
"mo"	"mo<u>r</u>e"
"fa"	"fa<u>r</u>"
"motha"	"mothe<u>r</u>"
"ha"	"he<u>r</u>"

Word Pairs for Practice

Make sure you don't pronounce these pairs of words the same:

no *r*	*r*
1. foam	form
2. moaning	morning
3. pot	part
4. tone	torn
5. cone	corn

The /l/ Sound

Make sure you don't quickly release the tip of your tongue for the *l* at the end of words. This will cause you to over-pronounce the /l/. The American /l/ sound is softer and longer than the French, and the tip of the tongue is more relaxed. Review the exercises for the American /l/ sound in Chapter Four.

Pronouncing *ing*

Over-pronouncing *ing* is another common mistake French speakers make. Be sure not to release the /g/ sound in words that end with *ing*, such as *going* and *doing*. Review the rules for this sound in Chapter Four.

Vowels

It is recommended that you study all of the American vowel sounds in detail. (See Chapters One and Two.) However, pay special attention to the vowel sounds highlighted below which are the most problematic ones for French speakers of English.

The /eɪ/ Sound

The /eɪ/ sound (as in *take*) doesn't exist in French, so French speakers generally pronounce it as /ɛ/. Thus, the words *take* and *tech* end up sounding the same. Pay special attention to this vowel sound when it's at the end of words. Listen to the way that Americans pronounce French words such as *fiancé*, *resumé* and *bouquet*. You will hear two vowel sounds at the end. For the word *stay*, instead of "sté," say "steiii."

Word Contrasts for Practice

Make sure that you pronounce the words in each pair differently:

/ɛ/	/eɪ/
1. wet	wait
2. west	waste
3. test	taste
4. men	main

The /ɔ/ Sound

Be careful that your /ɔ/ sound (as in *saw*) is not influenced by the very different British version of this sound. In British English *pause* sounds almost like "pose," but in American English it sounds much more like /pɑz/, and has the same /ɑ/ sound as in *father* or *watch*.

Word Contrasts for Practice

Make sure you pronounce the words in each pair differently.

/oʊ/	/ɔ/
1. low	law
2. boat	bought
3. coat	caught
4. woke	walk

The /ɪ/ Sound

You might have a tendency to pronounce /ɪ/ (as in *sit*) incorrectly. Make sure you pronounce the following words differently:

/ɪ/	/i/
1. sit	seat
2. live	leave
3. fill	feel

The /ə/ Sound

You might confuse /ə/ as in *fun*, with /ɑ/ as in *hop*. Practice pronouncing the following words differently:

/ɑ/	/ə/
1. shot	shut
2. lock	luck
3. cop	cup

The /ʊ/ Sound

Do not make the common error of confusing /ʊ/ as in *good*, with /u/ as in *food*. Make sure you pronounce the following words differently:

/ʊ/	/u/
1. full	fool
2. pull	pool
3. look	Luke

Similar Words in French and English

One of the biggest challenges for French speakers is the fact that there are many same or very similar words in English and French. Beware! Usually they are pronounced quite differently. People may have a hard time understanding you if say them with French pronunciation. Usually the difference is in syllable stress and vowel sound. You must simply get into the habit of looking up the pronunciation of these words and listening to native speakers of English.

Here is a sample of some of these words that exist in both languages but have different pronunciations. Test yourself by saying them in English. If you are not sure about their pronunciation, look them up in an audio dictionary.

develop	science
subject	professor
depend	specific
services	normal
realize	important

Syllable Stress

Chapter Five is particularly important for native French speakers. It will make you aware of the big differences between the rules of French and English word stress and vowel reduction. Review the explanations and exercises there.

Word Stress

In French, speakers stress the adjective more than the noun. In English it's the opposite. It's especially important for you to study all the rules of word stress in Chapter Six.

typical mistake:

"That's a **nice** car."
"He's an **intelligent** man."

should be:

"That's a nice **car**."
"He's an intelligent **man**."

Similarly, in French one tends to stress the first content word of a phrase or a sentence; in English the last content word gets the most stress.

typical mistake:

"I **drove** my car."
"I **went** to the bank."

should be:

"I drove my <u>**car**</u>."
"I went to the <u>**bank**</u>."

Other common word stress errors:

typical mistake:

"I **should** go."
"**Turn** it off."
"**U**CLA"

should be:

"I should <u>**go**</u>."
"Turn it <u>**off**</u>."
"UCL<u>**A**</u>"

Study all of the other rules of word stress in Chapters Five through Eight and practice the exercises over and over.

Intonation

There's a tendency for French speakers to use rising intonation or wavering intonation. Study the rules of intonation in Chapter Seven. Wrong intonation can make you sound hesitant, doubtful, or even sarcastic.

German

Study the whole book, but also pay special attention to the topics outline below. These highlight the common difficulties for native German speakers.

Consonants

Voiced and Voiceless Consonants

Review voiced and voiceless consonants in Chapter Three. There is a tendency for German speakers to change the final voiced consonant into a voiceless one, often at the ends of words.

common mistake:	should be:
"fi**f**e"	fi**v**e

Word Contrasts for Practice

Make sure you pronounce the following words in each pair differently.

voiceless	voiced
/k/	/g/
1. ba**ck**	ba**g**
2. pi**ck**	pi**g**
/ʧ/	/ʤ/
3. ri**ch**	ri**dge**
4. ba**tch**	ba**dge**
/t/	/d/
5. be**t**	be**d**
6. go**t**	Go**d**
/s/	/z/
7. pla**ce**	play**s**
8. pri**ce**	pri**ze**
/f/	/v/
9. sa**fe**	sa**ve**
10. proo**f**	pro**ve**

Confusing /s/ and /z/ Sounds

The *s* in many English words is frequently pronounced as a /z/ sound. Refer to the list in Chapter Four of common words with a /z/ sound. Other words pronounced with a /z/ sound include: *hu**s**band, de**s**ign, ob**s**erve, alway**s**,* and *cho**s**e.*

Confusing /v/ and /w/

All explanations and exercises for the /v/ and /w" sounds are in Chapter Four.

typical mistake:	*should be:*
"<u>v</u>ine"	"<u>w</u>ine"
"very <u>v</u>ell"	"very <u>w</u>ell"

The /l/ Sound

Make sure you don't quickly release the tip of your tongue for the *l* at the end of words. This will cause you to over-pronounce the /l/. The American /l/ sound is softer and longer than the German /l/, and the tip of the tongue is more relaxed. Review the exercises for the American /l/ sound in Chapter Four.

The *th* Sound

Review Chapters Three and Four to learn the correct pronunciation of this sound. A common mistake is to substitute /t/ or /d/ for *th*. Some German speakers may also substitute an *s* or *z* for *th*.

typical mistake:	*should be:*
"tank"	"<u>th</u>ank"
"dose"	"<u>th</u>ose"
"mudder"	"mo<u>th</u>er"

Word Pairs for Practice

Make sure that you don't pronounce the words in each pair the same way:

s	*th*
1. mass	math
2. pass	path
3. seem	theme
4. all so	although

The /r/ Sound

When it appears at the end of a word or before another consonant, the /r/ sound may pose some difficulties for the native German speaker. Review the explanations and exercises for the /r/ sound in Chapter Four. Make sure you pronounce the final /r/ at the end of words.

typical mistake:	*should be:*
"mo"	"mo<u>r</u>e"
"fa"	"fa<u>r</u>"
"motha"	"mothe<u>r</u>"
"ha"	"he<u>r</u>"

Word Pairs for Practice
Make sure you don't pronounce these pairs of words the same:

no *r*	*r*
1. foam	form
2. moaning	morning
3. pot	part
4. tone	torn
5. cone	corn

Vowels

It is recommended that you study all of the American vowel sounds in detail. (See Chapters One and Two.) However, pay special attention to the vowel sounds highlighted below which are the most problematic ones for German speakers of English.

Confusing /æ/ and /ɛ/

You might have a tendency to confuse /æ/ (as in *bad*) with /ɛ/ (as in *bed*.) If so, you will want to review the explanations and many exercises for these sounds in Chapters One and Two. A typical mistake would be to pronounce *sand* and *send* the same way.

Word Contrasts for Practice
Make sure you pronounce the words in each pair differently.

/æ/	/ɛ/
1. flash	flesh
2. man	men
3. salary	celery
4. ex	axe
5. taxes	Texas

The /ɔ/ Sound

Be careful that your /ɔ/ sound (as in *saw*) is not influenced by the very different British version of this sound. In British English *pause* sounds almost like "pose," but in American English it sounds much more like /pɑz/, and has the same /ɑ/ sound as in *father* or *watch*.

Word Contrasts for Practice
Make sure you pronounce the words in each pair differently:

/oʊ/	/ɔ/
1. low	law
2. boat	bought
3. coat	caught
4. woke	walk

The /ɪ/ Sound
You might have a tendency to pronounce /ɪ/ (as in *sit*) incorrectly. Make sure you pronounce the following words differently:

/ɪ/	/i/
1. sit	seat
2. live	leave
3. fill	feel

The /ə/ Sound
You might confuse /ə/ as in *fun*, with /ɑ/ as in *hop*. Practice pronouncing the following words differently:

/ɑ/	/ə/
1. shot	shut
2. lock	luck
3. cop	cup

The /ʊ/ Sound
Do not make the common error of confusing /ʊ/ as in *good*, with /u/ as in *food*. Make sure you pronounce the following words differently:

/ʊ/	/u/
1. full	fool
2. pull	pool
3. look	Luke

Indian Languages

Study the whole book, but also pay special attention to the topics outlined below. These are common areas of difficulty for Indian students of English.

Consonants

The /v/ Sound

You may have a tendency to confuse the /v/ and /w/ sounds. Be sure to review the explanations and exercises for these sounds in Chapter Four.

typical mistake:	*should be:*
"ha**we**"	"ha**ve**"
"**w**est"	"**v**est"

Dropping the *v* in the middle or at the end of a word is also a common mistake.

common mistake:	*should be:*
"fai dollars"	"fi**v**e dollars"
"goment"	"go**v**ernment"
"involed"	"invol**v**ed"

Practice Sentences

1. I ha**v**e to ha**v**e fi**v**e.
2. He will pro**v**e that he can impro**v**e the go**v**ernment.
3. I ha**v**e been invol**v**ed with them for ele**v**en or twel**v**e years.

The /r/ Sound

Learn to create the correct American /r/ sound by studying Chapter Three and by doing all of the /r/ exercises in Chapter Four. Make sure you do not roll the /r/ with the tip of your tongue, as this creates a harsh sounding Indian /r./

Indian speakers tend to roll the /r/ when it is followed by another consonant, as in *b**r**ing, p**r**ogram, f**r**iend,* or when it is in the beginning of the word as in ***r**ed* and ***r**ight.*

When the /r/ sound is at the end of the word, as in *fa**r*** and *compute**r**,* or before another consonant, as in *da**r**k* and *conce**r**t,* Indian speakers tend not to pronounce it at all. Remember, the /r/ is *never* silent in Standard American English whereas in British English it sometimes is.

typical mistake:	*should be:*
"mo"	"mo**r**e"
"fa"	"fa**r**"
"motha"	"mothe**r**"
"ha"	"he**r**"

Word Pairs for Practice

Make sure you don't pronounce these pairs of words the same:

no *r*	*r*
1. foam	form
2. moaning	morning
3. pot	part
4. tone	torn
5. cone	corn

The *th* Sound

Review Chapters Three and Four to learn the correct pronunciation of this sound. A common mistake is to substitute a /t/ or a /d/ for the *th*.

typical mistake:	*should be:*
"tank"	"<u>th</u>ank"
"dose"	"<u>th</u>ose"
"mudder"	"mo<u>th</u>er"

Vowels

It is recommended that you study all of the American vowel sounds in detail. (See Chapters One and Two.) However, pay special attention to the vowel sounds highlighted below which are the most problematic ones for Indian speakers of English.

The /eɪ/ Sound

Indian speakers tend to pronounce /eɪ/ (as in *take*) as /ɛ/ or /æ/, so the word *same* ends up sounding like *Sam.* Here are some other examples of words that tend to sound the same when Indian speakers pronounce them:

typical mistake:	*should be:*
/ɛ/	/eɪ/
"tech"	"take"
"sell"	"sale"
"test"	"taste"
"west"	"waste"

Confusing /ɛ/ and /æ/

Reiview Chapters One and Two to master the differences between /ɛ/ as in *bet* and /æ/ as in *bat.*

/æ/	/ɛ/
1. flash	flesh
2. man	men
3. salary	celery
4. ex	axe
5. taxes	Texas
6. sand	send

The /ɔ/ Sound

Be careful that your /ɔ/ sound (as in *saw*) is not influenced by the very different British version of this sound. In British English *pause* sounds almost like "pose," but in American English it sounds much more like /paz/, and has the same /ɑ/ sound as in *father* or *watch*.

Word Contrasts for Practice

Make sure you don't pronounce the two words in each pair the same way:

/oʊ/	/ɔ/
1. low	law
2. boat	bought
3. coat	caught
4. woke	walk

Syllable Stress

The English spoken in India follows very different rules for syllable stress of words. Sometimes there seem to be no consistent rules, probably because of the many dialects in India that are influencing the evolution of spoken English. As a result, a variety of syllable stresses seems to be accepted. Once during an accent reduction lesson in the United States, three Indian software engineers were asked to give the correct syllable stress of the word *engineer*. Three different answers were given. One person was certain that the correct pronunciation was "**en**gineer;" another student stated, "en**gin**eer;" and the third said, "engin**eer.**"

If you speak fast and you make these types of mistakes, it will certainly be difficult for people to understand you. Learn the correct syllable stress of the words that you most commonly use. Mark the syllable that you believe should be stressed and then check your answers in the dictionary. The most common mistake is to stress the first syllable.

Here is a sample list of words that Indian speakers commonly pronounce with the wrong stress. First test out your knowledge of these words by marking the syllable that you think should be stressed, and then check your dictionary or ask a native speaker for the correct answers.

1. although	9. Europe	17. agree	25. understand
2. sophisticated	10. combination	18. variety	26. determine
3. information	11. efficient	19. eliminate	27. development
4. discuss	12. instead	20. consist	28. economical
5. develop	13. response	21. priority	29. technique
6. register	14. spontaneous	22. penalty	30. concern
7. communication	15. exactly	23. whenever	31. request
8. idea	16. colleague	24. beginning	32. already

Word Stress

Indians tend to place the most stress in the first part of a phrase or sentence, whereas Americans stress the endings more. Remember to place the most emphasis on the last content word of each sentence. Review Chapter Six for more guidance on this topic.

common mistake:	*should be:*
"**Nice** to meet you."	"Nice to **meet** you."
"Have a **nice** day."	"Have a nice **day**."
"**I** have a car."	"I have a **car**."
"I **don't** know."	"I don't **know**."

Intonation

There's a tendency for Indian speakers to use rising or wavering intonation. Study the rules in Chapter Seven to work on this area.

Fast Speech

Indian speakers tend to speak very quickly and with a very different sentence melody. Combine that with mispronouncing some consonants and vowels, and you have a strong accent that can be difficult for Americans to understand. It is important for you to practice Chapters Five through Eight in order to master the rhythm and melody of English. Stressing content words will also help you to slow down your speech since you will be required to prolong the stressed vowels.

Indonesian

Study the whole book, but also pay special attention to the topics outline below. These are common areas of difficulty for Indonesian students of English.

Consonants

The *th* Sound
Review Chapters Three and Four to learn the correct pronunciation of this sound. A common mistake is to substitute a /t/ or a /d/ for the *th*.

typical mistake:	*should be:*
"tank"	"<u>th</u>ank"
"dose"	"<u>th</u>ose"
"mudder"	"mo<u>th</u>er"

Voiced and Voiceless Consonants
Review voiced and voiceless consonants in Chapter Three. There is a tendency for Indonesian speakers to change a voiced consonant into a voiceless one.

Words Contrasts for Practice
Make sure you pronounce the words in each pair differently.

f	*v*
1. li<u>fe</u>	li<u>ve</u>
2. <u>f</u>airy	<u>v</u>ery
3. <u>f</u>ew	<u>v</u>iew

Words Contrasts for Practice
Pronounce the two words in each pair differently

voiceless	voiced	voiceless	voiced
1. ba<u>ck</u>	ba<u>g</u>	5. be<u>t</u>	be<u>d</u>
2. go<u>t</u>	Go<u>d</u>	6. pla<u>ce</u>	play<u>s</u>
3. hal<u>f</u>	ha<u>ve</u>	7. bol<u>t</u>	bol<u>d</u>
4. hear<u>t</u>	har<u>d</u>	8. ri<u>ch</u>	ri<u>dge</u>

Confusing /s/ and /z/
The *s* in many English words is frequently pronounced as a /z/ sound. Learn the rules for this sound, and refer to the list of common words with a /z/ sound in Chapter Four. Other words pronounced with a /z/ sound include: *hu<u>s</u>band, de<u>s</u>ign, ob<u>s</u>erve, alway<u>s</u>,* and *cho<u>s</u>e.*

Words Contrasts for Practice
Make sure you say the words in each pair differently:

/s/	/z/
1. <u>S</u>ue	<u>z</u>oo
2. <u>S</u>ack	<u>Z</u>ack
3. pie<u>c</u>e	pea<u>s</u>
4. fa<u>c</u>e	pha<u>s</u>e

Consonant Clusters
When a word contains two consonants next to each other, make sure you pronounce both of the consonants. Review Chapter Four for more help with consonant clusters.

Words for Practice
Pronounce *both* of the final consonants in the words below:

1. ju<u>st</u>	6. proje<u>ct</u>
2. a<u>ct</u>	7. mi<u>xed</u>
3. lo<u>st</u>	8. pai<u>nt</u>
4. ha<u>nd</u>	9. se<u>nse</u>
5. pai<u>nt</u>	10. de<u>sks</u>

Confusing /v/ and /w/
All explanations and exercises for the /v/ and /w/ sounds are in Chapter Four.

common mistake:	*should be:*
"<u>v</u>ine"	"<u>w</u>ine"
"very <u>v</u>ell"	"very <u>w</u>ell"

The Initial *h*
Make sure you pronounce the /h/ sound at the beginning of words. The *h* is always pronounced in English except in these common words: *hour, honest, honor, herb, heir, exhaust, vehicle,* and *ghost.*

common mistake:	*should be:*
"she as"	"she <u>h</u>as"
"uman"	"<u>h</u>uman"

The /r/ Sound
Learn to create the correct American /r/ sound by studying Chapter Three and by doing all of the /r/ exercises in Chapter Four. Make sure you do not roll the /r/ with the tip of your tongue, as this creates a harsh sounding Indonesian /r/.

Indonesian speakers tend to roll the /r/ when it is followed by another consonant, as in *b<u>r</u>ing, p<u>r</u>ogram, f<u>r</u>iend,* or when it is in the beginning of the word, as in <u>r</u>ed and <u>r</u>ight.

When the /r/ sound is at the end of the word, as in *far* and *computer*, or before another consonant, as in *dark* and *concert*, Indonesian speakers tend not to pronounce it at all. Remember, the /r/ is *never* silent in Standard American English whereas in British English it sometimes is.

typical mistake:	*should be:*
"mo"	"mo*re*"
"fa"	"fa*r*"
"motha"	"mothe*r*"
"ha"	"he*r*"

Word Pairs for Practice

Make sure you don't pronounce these pairs of words the same:

no *r*	*r*
1. foam	form
2. moaning	morning
3. pot	part
4. tone	torn
5. cone	corn

Confusing *s* and *sh*

Indonesians tend to pronounce an /s/ sound when a word contains the letters *sh*. Common words that pose this problem include *finish*, *decision*, *physician*, *wish*, and *cash*.

Words Contrasts for Practice

Make sure that you pronounce the words in each pair below differently:

"s"	"sh"
1. see	she
2. seat	sheet
3. bass	bash

Vowels

It is recommended that you study all of the American vowel sounds in detail. (See Chapters One and Two.) However, pay special attention to the vowel sounds highlighted below which are the most problematic ones for Indonesian speakers of English.

The /eɪ/ Sound

Indonesian speakers tend to pronounce /eɪ/ (as in *take*) as /ɛ/ or /æ/, so the word *same* ends up sounding like *Sam*. Here are some other examples of words that tend to sound the same when Indonesian speakers pronounce them:

common mistake:	*should be:*
/ɛ/	/eɪ/
"tech"	"take"
"sell"	"sale"
"test"	"taste"
"west"	"waste"

The /ɑ/ Sound

Be careful about words spelled with an *o* but pronounced with an /ɑ/ sound, as in *father*. Common words in this category include: *job*, *hot*, *God*, *problem*, and *possible*.

Syllable Stress

Study Chapter Five to review the rules of syllable stress. Your tendency will be to stress the first syllable of a word. If you speak quickly and use the wrong syllable stress, your speech will be difficult to understand.

Word Stress

Indonesians tend to place the most stress in the first part of a phrase or sentence, whereas Americans stress the endings more. Remember to place the most emphasis on the last content word of each sentence. Review Chapter Six for more guidance on this topic.

common mistake:	*should be:*
"**Nice** to meet you."	"Nice to **meet** you."
"Have a **nice** day."	"Have a nice **day**."
"**I** have a car."	"I have a **car.**"
"I **don't** know."	"I don't **know**."

Japanese

Study the whole book, but also pay special attention to the topics outlined below. These are common areas of difficulty for Japanese speakers of English.

Consonants

The /r/ Sound

Learn to pronounce the correct American /r/ sound by studying Chapter Three and by doing all the /r/ exercises in Chapter Four.

When the /r/ sound is at the end of the word, as in *far* and *computer*, or before another consonant, as in *dark* and *concert*, Japanese speakers tend not to pronounce it at all. Remember, the /r/ is *never* silent in Standard American English whereas in British English it sometimes is.

typical mistake:	*should be:*
"mo"	"mo<u>r</u>e"
"fa"	"fa<u>r</u>"
"motha"	"mothe<u>r</u>"
"ha"	"he<u>r</u>"

Word Pairs for Practice

Make sure you don't pronounce these pairs of words the same:

no *r*	*r*
1. foam	form
2. moaning	morning
3. pot	part
4. tone	torn
5. cone	corn

Native Japanese speakers tend to confuse the /r/ and /l/ sounds. Study Chapter Three to learn the difference between these two sounds, and do all of the *r* and *l* exercises in Chapter Four. Be especially careful about the *r* and *l* when they are near each other as in: *enti<u>r</u>e<u>l</u>y*, *<u>r</u>a<u>r</u>e<u>l</u>y*, and *ba<u>r</u>e<u>l</u>y*. Also take special care when they are preceded by another consonant as in *<u>f</u>ly* and *<u>f</u>ry*.

Confusing /f/ and /h/

The Japanese sound for *f* is a combination of the English /f/ and /h/. Be especially careful not to pronounce *fu* like "hu." Compare how an American and a Japanese person would pronounce the word *Fuji*. For the American /f/, make sure that your lower lip is touching your upper teeth.

Confusing /b/ and /v/

Review the exercises in Chapter Four. Remember, the /b/ sound requires the lips to be completely closed, with no air coming out, whereas the /v/ sound only involves the lower lip, which touches the upper teeth and creates a vibrating air flow. Be particularly careful with words that contain both a *b* and *v* or when these sounds are close together, as in *Beverly, November, vibrate, available, I've been* and *very big*.

The /w/ Sound

Review the section on the /w/ sound in Chapter Four. Make sure that you are producing a puff of air and that your vocal cords are vibrating as you produce this sound. Don't say "I us," say "I was." Pay special attention to the *w* in the middle of words and to words that begin with *qu*. Remember, *qu* sounds like /kw/ as in *question*. Don't say "/kɛs/ + tion," say "/kwes/ + tion."

Here are some commonly mispronounced words with a /w/ sound:

1. twelve	5. someone (one = "won")	9. somewhere
2. forward	6. always	10. overwhelmed
3. question	7. would	11. quiet
4. quit	8. inquire	12. language (u = /w/)

Confusing /ʒ/ and /ʤ/

Both the /ʒ/ sound (as in *beige*) and the /ʤ/ sound (as in *orange*) are voiced. The easiest way to fix the problem of confusing these two sounds is to practice pronouncing their voiceless pairs. First say the *sh* sound as in *shoes* and then add the vibration to the vocal cords. That will produce the /ʒ/ sound. Now say the *ch* sound as in *choose*. If you add vibration and make it voiced, that produces the /ʤ/ sound. So, if you can pronounce *shoes* and *choose* differently, you can also pronounce *massage* (/ʒ/) and *message* (/ʤ/) differently.

The *th* sound

Review Chapters Three and Four to learn the correct pronunciation of this sound. A common mistake is to substitute a /t/ or a /d/ for *th*.

common mistake:	*should be:*
"tank"	"thank"
"dose"	"those"
"mudder"	"mother"

Some Japanese speakers also substitute an "s" or "z" for "th."

Word Contrasts for Practice

Make sure that you don't pronounce these words the same:

s	*th*
1. mass	math
2. pass	path
3. seem	theme
4. all so	although

Common Vowel Errors

The "ar" words

When the /ɑ/ sound is followed by /r/, it is pronounced incorrectly by many Japanese speakers. The /ɑ/ requires the tongue to lie flat at the bottom of the mouth and the jaw to be wide open; then the tongue must be quickly curled up to move into the /r/ position. This type of unfamiliar tongue movement can be quite a challenge for Japanese speakers. Usually one of these sounds ends up being compromised and the word *farm* ends sounding either like "firm" or "fam." You need to work on clearly pronouncing both sounds.

Word Contrasts for Practice

Make sure you pronounce the words in each pair below differently:

/ɚ/	/ɑr/
1. heard	hard
2. firm	farm
3. fir	far
4. stir	star
5. perk	park

Practice Sentences

1. I will park my car in his yard.
2. His large apartment is not very far.
3. Mark played his guitar in the dark bar.
4. Marshall Clark will start in March.
5. I paid for the seminar with my charge card.

The /ɔ/ Sound

Be careful that your /ɔ/ sound (as in *saw*) is not influenced by the very different British version of this sound. In British English *pause* sounds almost like "pose," but in American English it sounds much more like /pɑz/, and has the same /ɑ/ sound as in *father* or *watch*.

Word Contrasts for Practice

Make sure you don't pronounce the two words in each pair the same way:

/oʊ/	/ɔ/
1. low	law
2. boat	bought
3. coat	caught
4. woke	walk

The /ɪ/ Sound

You might have a tendency to pronounce /ɪ/ (as in *sit*) incorrectly. Make sure you pronounce the following words differently:

/ɪ/	/i/
1. sit	seat
2. live	leave
3. fill	feel

The /ə/ Sound

You might confuse /ə/ as in *fun*, with /ɑ/ as in *hop*. Practice pronouncing the following words differently:

/ɑ/	/ə/
1. shot	shut
2. lock	luck
3. cop	cup

The /ʊ/ Sound

Do not make the common error of confusing /ʊ/ as in *good*, with /u/ as in *food*. Make sure you pronounce the following words differently:

/ʊ/	/u/
1. full	fool
2. pull	pool
3. look	Luke

Korean

Study the whole book, but also pay special attention to the topics outlined below. These are common areas of difficulty for Korean speakers of English.

Consonants

Confusing /r/ and /l/

Study Chapter Three to learn the difference between these two sounds and do all of the *r* and *l* exercises in Chapter Four. Be especially careful about the *r* and *l* when they are near each other as in: *entirely, rarely,* and *barely.*

Pronouncing Both /n/ + /l/

Because a similar tongue position is used to pronounce both /n/ and /l/, there is a tendency for Koreans to pronounce them as one when they are next to each other. Make sure you clearly pronounce both sounds in the following words:

    un<u>l</u>ess   o<u>nl</u>y   sudde<u>nl</u>y   mai<u>nl</u>y

The /w/ Sound

Review the section on the /w/ sound in Chapter Four. Make sure that you are producing a puff of air and that your vocal cords are vibrating as you produce this sound. Don't say "I us," say "I <u>w</u>as." Pay special attention to the *w* in the middle of words and to words that begin with *qu*. Remember, *qu* sounds like /kw/ as in *question*. Don't say "/kes/ + tion," say "/k<u>w</u>es/ + tion."

Here are some commonly mispronounced words with a /w/ sound:

1. t<u>w</u>elve	5. some<u>o</u>ne (one = "<u>w</u>on")	9. some<u>w</u>here
2. for<u>w</u>ard	6. al<u>w</u>ays	10. over<u>w</u>helmed
3. q<u>u</u>estion	7. <u>w</u>ould	11. q<u>u</u>iet
4. q<u>u</u>it	8. inq<u>u</u>ire	12. lang<u>u</u>age (u = /w/)

Confusing /b/ and /v/

Review the exercises in Chapter Four. Remember, the /b/ sound requires the lips to be completely closed, with no air coming out, whereas the /v/ sound only involves the lower lip, which touches the upper teeth and creates a vibrating air flow. Be particularly careful with words that contain both a *b* and *v* or when these sounds are close together as in: *<u>Beverly</u>, <u>November</u>, <u>vibrate</u>, a<u>v</u>aila<u>b</u>le, I'<u>v</u>e <u>b</u>een,* and *<u>very big</u>.*

Confusing /p/ and /f/

Because the /f/ does not exist in Korean, there is a tendency to put the lips together and form a /p/ sound instead. This type of mistake is parallel to the /v/ and /b/ confusion, and it requires you to focus on using either two lips or just the lower lip. Be particularly careful with words that contain both a *p* and an *f* or when these two sounds are close together as in: *<u>perfect</u>, <u>perform</u>, <u>puffy</u>, hel<u>pf</u>ul, <u>full page</u>,* and *cu<u>p</u> of co<u>ff</u>ee.*

Word Contrasts for Practice

Make sure you pronounce the words in each pair below differently.

/p/	/f/
1. pore	for
2. pup	puff
3. cups	cuffs
4. plight	flight
5. a pair	a fair
6. praise	phrase

Practice Sentences

1. That's a perfect performance.
2. I will pay up front for the fans.
3. I prefer to have coffee before five pm.
4. Do you feel that I improved my French?

Confusing /z/ and /ʤ/

The following words all have a /z/ sound but they are commonly mispronounced with a /ʤ/ sound. Review Chapter Three which discusses the correct tongue positions for these sounds.

disease	zoo	business	transition
physician	thousand	desire	result
design	busy	exaggerate*	exist*

*The *x* in the words *exaggerate* and *exist* is pronounced as /gz/.

Word Contrasts for Practice

Make sure you pronounce the words in each pair below differently.

/ʤ/	/z/
1. Jew	zoo
2. budging	buzzing
3. jealous	zealous
4. range	rains

Confusing /ʒ/ and /ʤ/

Both the /ʒ/ (as in *beige*) and the /ʤ/ sound (as in *orange*) are voiced. The easiest way to fix the problem of confusing these two sounds is to practice pronouncing their voiceless pairs. First say the *sh* sound as in *shoes* and then add the vibration to the vocal cords. That will produce the /ʒ/ sound. Now say the *ch* sound as in *choose*. If you add vibration and make it voiced, that produces the /ʤ/ sound. So, if you can pronounce <u>sh</u>oes and <u>ch</u>oose differently, you can also pronounce *massage* (/ʒ/) and *message* (/ʤ/) differently. Below are a few common words with the /ʒ/ sound:

usual	beige	Asian	garage
prestige	vision	occasion	regime

The *th* sound

Review Chapters Three and Four to learn the correct pronunciation of this sound. A common mistake is to substitute a /t/ or a /d/ for *th*.

common mistake:	*should be:*
"tank"	"<u>th</u>ank"
"dose"	"<u>th</u>ose"
"mudder"	"mo<u>th</u>er"

Vowels

It is recommended that you study all of the American vowel sounds in detail. (See Chapters One and Two.) However, pay special attention to the vowel sounds highlighted below.

Confusing /æ/ and /ɛ/

The sounds /æ/ (as in *bad*) and /ɛ/ (as in *bed*) are often confused by native Korean speakers. Review Chapters One and Two for more explanations and exercises related to these sounds.

Word Contrasts for Practice

Make sure you pronounce the words in each pair below differently.

/æ/	/ɛ/
1. flash	flesh
2. man	men
3. salary	celery
4. ex	axe
5. taxes	Texas
6. sand	send

The /ɔ/ Sound

Be careful that your /ɔ/ sound (as in *saw*) is not influenced by the very different British version of this sound. In British English *pause* sounds almost like "pose," but in American English it sounds much more like /pɑz/, and has the same /ɑ/ sound as in *father* or *watch*.

Word Contrasts for Practice

Don't pronounce the two words in each pair the same way.

/oʊ/	/ɔ/
1. low	law
2. boat	bought
3. coat	caught
4. woke	walk

Syllable Stress

There is a tendency for Koreans to stress the first syllable of words. Review Chapter Five on syllable stress and continuously practice saying longer words while checking that you are stressing the right syllable. Don't assume the first syllable is the one to be stressed.

typical mistake:

1. "**spe**cific"
2. "**sta**tistics"
3. "**com**petition"
4. "**fa**miliar"
5. "**se**cure"
6. "**when**ever"
7. "**pro**fession"
8. "**con**sultant"

should be:

"spe**ci**fic"
"sta**ti**stics"
"compe**ti**tion"
"fa**mi**liar"
"sec**ure**"
"when**ev**er"
"pro**fes**sion"
"con**sul**tant"

Word Stress

Just as Koreans tend to stress the first syllable of a word, they also tend to stress the first word of each sentence. Try to break this pattern. Practice the rules of word stress as outlined in Chapters Six and Seven.

common mistake:

1. "**I** agree."
2. "**My** name is…"

should be:

"I **agree**."
"My **name** is… ."

Portuguese

Study the whole book, but also pay special attention to the topics outlined below. These are common areas of difficulty for native Portuguese speakers.

Consonants

The Final *l*

The Portuguese final *l* sounds almost like the English /w/ or /ou/ sound. Practice the *l* exercises in Chapter Four. Make sure that the tip of your tongue is touching the gum ridge behind your upper teeth.

typical mistake:	*should be:*
"Ca<u>w</u> me"	"ca<u>ll</u> me"
"bow"	"bow<u>l</u>"

The /s/ Sound

The Portuguese language has no word that begins with an *s* followed by another consonant. There is usually a vowel in front of the *s*. Make sure you don't inadvertently insert an extra vowel sound when you say English words beginning with *s*. Here are some common words that demonstrate the "*s* problem."

Portuguese:	*English (no vowel in front):*
<u>es</u>cola	<u>s</u>chool
<u>Es</u>panhol	<u>Sp</u>anish
<u>es</u>tudar	<u>st</u>udy
<u>es</u>pecial	<u>sp</u>ecial

The *th* sound

Review Chapters Three and Four to learn the correct pronunciation of this sound. A common mistake is to substitute /t/ or /d/ for *th*.

common mistake:	*should be:*
"tank"	"<u>th</u>ank"
"dose"	"<u>th</u>ose"
"mudder"	"mo<u>th</u>er"

Consonant Clusters

Practice all of the exercises on consonant clusters in Chapter Four. In the Portuguese language, when there are two consonants together, such as *rd* or *ct*, a vowel usually follows. In English that is not the case. For example, Americans say "Robe<u>rt</u>" with *rt* at the end. The Portuguese equivalent is "Robe<u>rto.</u>" Here the *rt* cluster is followed by a vowel, making it easier to pronounce the second consonant. Because it doesn't feel natural for Portuguese speakers to pronounce the consonant at the end, they tend to pronounce only the first consonant of the group, making the name *Robert* sound like "robbe<u>r</u>." Also, *ca<u>rd</u>* can sound like "ca<u>r</u>," and *Richa<u>rd</u>* will sound like "riche<u>r.</u>" Another good example is the English word *corre<u>ct</u>*, which in Portuguese is *corre<u>to</u>*.

When you come across a word with two or more consonants next to each other, make sure that you pronounce *every* consonant. Pay special attention to past tense *-ed* verbs. They generally form consonant clusters as in "wor**ked**" and "wat**ched.**"

Verbs Ending in *-ed*

Make sure you learn to pronounce the three different *-ed* endings of verbs. For example, the endings of the verbs *needed, opened,* and *passed* are all pronounced differently. Review Chapter Four for more guidance on this topic.

Word Pairs for Practice

1. wor**ked** ha**rd**
2. e**xtr**a **strength**
3. lo**st** and fou**nd**
4. play**ed** ca**rds**
5. e**xtr**emely difficu**lt**
6. wi**ld** wo**rld**

Vowels

It is recommended that you study all of the American vowel sounds in detail. (See Chapters One and Two.) However, pay special attention to the vowel sounds highlighted below which are the most problematic ones for native Portuguese speakers.

Confusing /æ/ and /ɛ/

The sounds /æ/ (as in *bad*) with /ɛ/ (as in *bed*) are often confused by native Portuguese speakers. Review Chapters One and Two for more explanations and exercises related to these sounds.

Word Contrasts for Practice

Make sure you pronounce the words in each pair below differently.

/æ/	/ɛ/
1. flash	flesh
2. man	men
3. salary	celery
4. ex	axe
5. taxes	Texas
6. sand	send

The /ɔ/ Sound

Be careful that your /ɔ/ sound (as in *saw*) is not influenced by the very different British version of this sound. In British English *pause* sounds almost like "pose," but in American English it sounds much more like /paz/, and has the same /ɑ/ sound as in *father* or *watch*.

Word Contrasts for Practice

Don't pronounce the two words in each pair the same way.

/oʊ/	/ɔ/
1. low	law
2. boat	bought
3. coat	caught
4. woke	walk

The /I/ Sound

You might have a tendency to pronounce /I/ (as in *sit*) incorrectly. Make sure you pronounce the following words differently:

/I/	/i/
1. sit	seat
2. live	leave
3. fill	feel

The /ə/ Sound

You might confuse /ə/ as in *fun*, with /ɑ/ as in *hop*. Practice pronouncing the following words differently:

/ɑ/	/ə/
1. shot	shut
2. lock	luck
3. cop	cup

The /ʊ/ Sound

Do not make the common error of confusing /ʊ/ as in *good*, with /u/ as in *food*. Make sure you pronounce the following words differently:

/ʊ/	/u/
1. full	fool
2. pull	pool
3. look	Luke

Reduced Vowels in Unstressed Syllables

In Portuguese vowels within unstressed syllables are pronounced fully, whereas in English they almost disappear and become a reduced schwa /ə/ sound. For further study and practice, refer to Chapter Five on syllable stress. Below are some examples of the vowel differences between the two languages.

Portuguese	English
dout<u>o</u>r	doctor – *sounds like "daktr"*
mét<u>o</u>do	method – *sounds like "methd"*
urb<u>a</u>no	urban – *sounds like "urbn"*

Word Stress

In Portuguese, adjectives are stressed more than nouns are. In English it's the opposite.

typical mistake:

"That's a **nice** car."

"He's an **intelligent** man."

should be:

"That's a nice **<u>car</u>**."

"He's an intelligent **<u>man.</u>**"

Similarly, Portuguese speakers tend to place the most stress in the first part of a phrase or sentence, whereas Americans stress the endings more. Remember to place the most emphasis on the last content word of each sentence. Review Chapter Six for more guidance on this topic.

typical mistake:

"I **drove** my car."

"I **went** to the bank."

should be:

"I drove my **<u>car</u>**."

"I went to the **<u>bank</u>**."

Other common word stress errors:

typical mistake:

"I **should** go."

"**Turn** it off."

"**U**CLA"

should be:

"I should **<u>go</u>**."

"Turn it **<u>off</u>**."

"UCL**<u>A</u>**"

Study all the rules of word stress in Chapters Five through Eight, and practice the exercises over and over.

Russian

Study the whole book, but also pay special attention to the topics outlined below. These are common areas of difficulty for native Russian speakers.

Consonants

Hard and Soft Consonants

Almost all Russian consonants come in hard/soft pairs. The soft consonant (Мягкий) is created by adding a sort of /y/ sound. In some common English words, Russian speakers tend to use the soft /n/ and /l/ when they are followed by the /i/ and /I/ vowel sounds—but /n/ and /l/ are almost always hard (Твёрдый) in English. To fix this common mistake, make sure you are using just the tip of your tongue to create the /n/ and the /l/ when they are followed by /i/ and /I/. If the middle of your tongue touches your gum ridge, it creates a soft consonant. Also, be careful not to use the soft /h/ after an /æ/ sound as in _have_ and _happy_. Again, this error has to do with how much of the surface of your tongue you are using to create the sound.

Words for Practice

Don't use a soft /n/ when pronouncing the following common words.

1. a**ny**	6. a**ny**thing
2. mo**ney**	7. **nea**r
3. ge**ne**ral	8. ma**ny**
4. Chi**ne**se	9. begi**nn**ing
5. commu**ni**cate	10. **Ni**ck

More Words for Practice

Don't use a soft /l/ with the following common words.

1. be**li**eve	3. rea**lly**
2. ana**ly**st	4. actua**lly**

Voiced and Voiceless Consonants

Review voiced and voiceless consonants in Chapter Three. There is a tendency for Russian speakers to change the final voiced consonant into a voiceless one.

common mistake:	*should be:*
"fi**f**e"	fi**v**e

Word Contrasts for Practice

Make sure you pronounce the two words in each pair below differently.

voiceless	voiced
/k/	/g/
1. ba**ck**	bag
2. pi**ck**	pig

/tʃ/	/dʒ/
3. ri<u>ch</u>	ri<u>dge</u>
4. bat<u>ch</u>	ba<u>dge</u>

/t/	/d/
5. be<u>t</u>	be<u>d</u>
6. go<u>t</u>	Go<u>d</u>

/s/	/z/
7. pla<u>c</u>e	play<u>s</u>
8. pri<u>c</u>e	pri<u>z</u>e

/f/	/v/
9. sa<u>f</u>e	sa<u>ve</u>
10. proo<u>f</u>	pro<u>ve</u>

The *th* sound

Review Chapters Three and Four to learn the correct pronunciation of this sound. A common mistake is to substitute a /t/ or a /d/ for *th*.

common mistake:	*should be:*
"tank"	"<u>th</u>ank"
"dose"	"<u>th</u>ose"
"mudder"	"mo<u>th</u>er"

Confusing /v/ and /w/

All explanations and exercises for the /v/ and /w/ sounds are in Chapter Four.

common mistake:	*should be:*
"<u>v</u>ine"	"<u>w</u>ine"
"very <u>v</u>ell"	"very <u>w</u>ell"

The /r/ sound

Learn to pronounce the correct American /r/ sound by studying Chapter Three, and by doing all the /r/ exercises in Chapter Four. Make sure you do not roll the /r/ with the tip of your tongue, as this creates a harsh sounding Russian /r/.

Russian speakers tend to roll the /r/ particularly when it is followed by another conso-nant, as in *b<u>r</u>ing, p<u>r</u>ogram, f<u>r</u>iend,* or when it is in the beginning of the word, as in *<u>r</u>ed* and *<u>r</u>ight*.

When the /r/ sound is at the end of the word, as in *fa<u>r</u>* and *compute<u>r</u>,* or before another consonant, as in *da<u>r</u>k* and *conce<u>r</u>t,* Russian speakers do not pronounce it at all. Remember, the /r/ is *never* silent in Standard American English, whereas in British English it some-times is.

	typical mistake:	*should be:*
	"mo"	"mo<u>re</u>"
	"fa"	"fa<u>r</u>"
	"motha"	"mothe<u>r</u>"
	"ha"	"he<u>r</u>"

Word Pairs for Practice

Make sure you don't pronounce these pairs of words the same:

no *r*	*r*
1. foam	form
2. moaning	morning
3. pot	part
4. tone	torn
5. cone	corn

Pronouncing *ing*

Over-pronouncing *ing* is another common mistake Russian speakers make. Be sure not to release the /g/ sound in words that end with *ing*, such as *going* and *doing*. Also make sure that you don't change the /g/ into a voiceless /k/ sound. Review the rules for this sound in Chapter Four.

Vowels

It is recommended that you study all of the American vowel sounds in detail. (See Chapters One and Two.) However, pay special attention to the vowel sounds highlighted below which are the most problematic for Russian speakers.

The /ɔ/ Sound

Be careful that your /ɔ/ sound (as in *saw*) is not influenced by the very different British version of this sound. In British English *pause* sounds almost like "pose," but in American English it sounds much more like /pɑz/, and has the same /ɑ/ sound as in *father* or *watch*.

Word Contrasts for Practice

Don't pronounce the two words in each pair below the same way.

/oʊ/	/ɔ/
1. low	law
2. boat	bought
3. coat	caught
4. woke	walk

Words Spelled with *o*

English words spelled with *o* are particularly difficult for Russian speakers since *o* is usually pronounced as /ɑ/ as in *stop* and *hot*, but it can also be pronounced as /ə/ as in *love* and *Monday* or even as /ou/ as in *so* and *only*.

Another common mistake is to pronounce a final *o* as /ə/ or /ɑ/. Make sure it's pronounced as /ou/ instead.

typical mistake:	*should be:*
/ɑ/	/ou/
"Mexic**a**"	"Mexic**o**"
"San Francisc**a**"	"San Francisc**o**"

The /I/ Sound

You might have a tendency to pronounce /I/ (as in *sit*) incorrectly. Make sure you pronounce the following words differently:

	/I/	/i/
1.	sit	seat
2.	live	leave
3.	fill	feel

The /ə/ Sound

You might confuse /ə/ as in *fun*, with /ɑ/ as in *hop*. Practice pronouncing the following words differently:

	/ɑ/	/ə/
1.	shot	shut
2.	lock	luck
3.	cop	cup

The /ʊ/ Sound

Do not make the common error of confusing /ʊ/ as in *good*, with /u/ as in *food*. Make sure you pronounce the following words differently:

	/ʊ/	/u/
1.	full	fool
2.	pull	pool
3.	look	Luke

Spanish

Study the whole book, but also pay special attention to the topics outlined below. These are common areas of difficulty for native Spanish speakers.

Consonants

Consonant Clusters

Practice all of the exercises on consonant clusters in Chapter Four. In the Spanish language, when there are two consonants together, such as *rd* or *ct*, a vowel usually follows. In English that is not the case. For example, Americans say *Robert* with "rt" at the end. The Spanish equivalent is "Robe*rto*"—the *rt* cluster is followed by a vowel, making it easier to pronounce the second consonant. Because it doesn't feel natural to Spanish speakers to pronounce the consonant at the end, they tend to pronounce only the first consonant of the group, making the name *Robert* sound like "robbe*r.*" Also, *card* can sound like "ca*r*," and *Richard* will sound like "riche*r.*" Another good example is the English word *correct*, which in Spanish is "corre*cto.*"

When you come across a word with two or more consonants next to each other, make sure that you pronounce *every* consonant. Pay special attention to past tense *-ed* verbs. They generally form consonant clusters as in *work**ed*** and *watch**ed***.

Word Pairs for Practice

Be sure to pronounce *every* consonant in the words below.

1. wo**rked** ha**rd**
2. ex**tr**a **strength**
3. lo**st** and fou**nd**
4. play**ed** ca**rds**
5. ex**tr**emely difficu**lt**
6. wi**ld** wo**rld**

Verbs Ending in *-ed*

Make sure you learn to pronounce the three different *-ed* endings of verbs. For example, the endings of the verbs *needed*, *opened*, and *passed* are all pronounced differently. Review Chapter Four for more guidance on this topic.

typical mistake:
"I work yesterday."

should be:
"I work**ed** yesterday."

The *th* Sound

Review Chapters Three and Four to learn the correct pronunciation of this sound. A common mistake is to substitute a /t/ or a /d/ for *th*.

common mistake:
"tank"
"dose"
"mudder"

should be:
"**th**ank"
"**th**ose"
"mo**th**er"

Confusing "b" and "v"

Because the Spanish *b* and *v* are pronounced the same, many Spanish speakers of English pronounce the words *very* and *berry* or *curve* and *curb* the same. You can practice these sounds in detail in Chapter Four.

Confusing /ʤ/ and /y/

The Spanish *ll* as in the words *silla*, is usually pronounced like the English /ʤ/ and/y/ put together or, in certain Spanish dialects, like the /y/ sound. You need to learn the difference between these two English sounds. Otherwise, you might end up saying "I'm going to jail," when you wanted to say "I'm going to Yale."

For the /ʤ/ sound, the tip of the tongue quickly touches the gum ridge and then releases. The sides of the tongue are against the upper teeth. For the /y/ sound, the tip of the tongue is down touching the bottom teeth.

Word Contrasts for Practice

Make sure you pronounce the two words in each pair differently.

/ʤ/	/y/
1. jet	yet
2. Jew	you
3. joke	yolk
4. jam	yam
5. major	mayor
6. juice	use

Confusing *sh* and *ch*

Remember, *sh* or /ʃ/ requires a continuous air flow coming out through the tongue. For the /tʃ/ sound (*ch*), however, the tip of the tongue blocks the air flow.

Word Contrasts for Practice

/ʃ/	/tʃ/
1. shoes	choose
2. share	chair
3. wash	watch
4. cash	catch
5. sheet	cheat
6. wish	witch
7. mash	match
8. washing	watching

Take note of the following exceptions. These words are spelling with *ch* but are pronounced with a *sh* or /ʃ/ sound. These words are mostly French in origin.

1. chef	4. chandelier	7. Chicago
2. machine	5. champagne	8. Michigan
3. chic	6. chauffeur	9. Chevrolet

1. a. Whi**ch** **sh**oes **sh**ould **sh**e **ch**oose?
   b. **Sh**e **sh**ould pur**ch**ase the **ch**eaper **sh**oes.

2. a. Where are **Sh**awn and **Ch**arlie?
   b. **Ch**arlie's in **ch**ur**ch** and **Sh**awn's in the kit**ch**en wa**sh**ing di**sh**es.

3. a. **Sh**ould I swit**ch** the **ch**annel?
   b. Don't swit**ch** the **ch**annel. I'm wat**ch**ing the **sh**ow.

4. a. What's the **ch**eapest way to **sh**ip the **ch**ips?
   b. It's mu**ch** **ch**eaper to **sh**ip the **ch**ips by **sh**ip.

5. a. These pea**ch**es are deli**ci**ous.
   b. Do you wi**sh** to **sh**are them with ea**ch** of us?

The /m/ Sound

When speaking quickly, Spanish speakers often don't fully close their lips to produce the /m/ sound especially when it is in the middle of or at the end of a word. Therefore, *From time to time* can end up sounding like: *fron tine to tine*. Also, the word *sometimes* can sound like *sonetine*. Make sure you don't confuse *m* with an /n/ sound.

Words for Practice

Be sure to fully pronounce the /m/ sound in the words below.

1. I'**m**	4. so**me**
2. fro**m**	5. ti**me**
3. so**metimes**	6. mini**mum**

The /s/ Sound

The Spanish language has no word that begins with an *s* followed by another consonant. There is usually a vowel in front of the *s*. Make sure you don't inadvertently insert an extra vowel sound when you say English words beginning with *s*. Here are some common words that demonstrate the *s* problem .

Spanish:	*English (no vowel in front):*
escuela	**sch**ool
español	**Sp**anish
estudiar	**st**udy
Esteban	**St**even

Confusing /s/ and /z/

The *s* in many English words is frequently pronounced as a /z/ sound. Learn the rules for this and refer to the list of common words with a /z/ sound in Chapter Four. Other words pronounced with a /z/ sound include *hu*ṣ*band, de*ṣ*ign, ob*ṣ*erve, alway*ṣ,* and cho*ṣ*e. Also, note that in Spanish, a *z* is pronounced as an /s/ sound. This is not the case in English.

Word Contrasts for Practice
Make sure you say the two words in each pair below differently.

/s/	/z/
1. piece	peas
2. face	phase
3. bus	buzz
4. price	prize

Vowels

Since Spanish has a lot fewer vowel sounds than English, you will need to review all of the American vowel sounds in Chapters One and Two. Also pay special attention to the vowel sounds highlighted below which are the most problematic ones for native Spanish speakers.

Words Spelled with *o*

English words spelled with *o* are particularly difficult for Spanish speakers since *o* is usually pronounced as /ɑ/ as in *stop* and *hot*, but it can also be pronounced as /ə/ as in *love* and *Monday* or even as /ou/ as in *so* and *only*. Study Chapter 2 in detail.

The /I/ Sound

You might have a tendency to pronounce /I/ (as in *sit*) incorrectly. Make sure you pronounce the following words differently:

/I/	/i/
1. sit	seat
2. live	leave
3. fill	feel

The /ə/ Sound

You might confuse /ə/ as in *fun*, with /ɑ/ as in *hop*. Practice pronouncing the following words differently:

/ɑ/	/ə/
1. shot	shut
2. lock	luck
3. cop	cup

The /ʊ/ Sound

Do not make the common error of confusing /ʊ/ as in *good*, with /u/ as in *food*. Make sure you pronounce the following words differently:

/ʊ/	/u/
1. full	fool
2. pull	pool
3. look	Luke

Reduced Vowels in Unstressed Syllables

In Spanish all the vowels are pronounced fully, whereas in English vowels in unstressed syllables almost disappear and become a reduced schwa /ə/ sound. For example, the word *doctor* exists in both languages. In Spanish both of the *o* sounds are pronounced the same way. In English, the word sounds like "doctr." The second *o* is changed to a short, reduced /ə/ sound because it's part of the unstressed syllable. For further study and practice, refer to Chapter Five on syllable stress. Below are some examples of the vowel differences between the two languages.

Spanish:	*English (no vowel in front):*
col<u>o</u>r	color – *sounds like "colr"*
norm<u>a</u>l	normal – *sounds like "norml"*
popul<u>a</u>r	popular – *sound like "populr"*

Word Stress

In Spanish, adjectives are stressed more than nouns are. In English it's the opposite.

typical mistake:	*should be:*
"That's a **nice** car."	"That's a nice **car**."
"He's an **intelligent** man."	"He's an intelligent **man.**"

Similarly, Spanish speakers tend to place the most stress in the first part of a phrase or sentence, whereas Americans stress the endings more. Remember to place the most emphasis on the last content word of each sentence. Review Chapter Six for more guidance on this topic.

typical mistake:	*should be:*
"I **drove** my car."	"I drove my **car**."
"I **went** to the bank."	"I went to the **bank**."

Other common word stress errors:

typical mistake:	*should be:*
"I **should** go."	"I should **go**."
"**Turn** it off."	"Turn it **off**."
"**U**CLA"	"UCL**A**"

Study all the rules of word stress in Chapters Five through Eight, and practice the exercises over and over.

Vietnamese

Study the whole book, but also pay special attention to the topics outlined below. These are common areas of difficulty for native Vietnamese speakers.

Consonants

Voiced and Voiceless Consonants

There is a tendency for Vietnamese speakers to change voiced consonants into voiceless ones. Review voiced and voiceless consonants in Chapter Three.

Pay special attention to words with *g* particularly when the *g* is followed by an *r* as in *great* and *graduate*. Make sure that you fully release the back of your tongue after it touches the back of the mouth so that the *g* can be clearly heard. Otherwise, *great* may sound like "crate" or even "rate."

typical mistake:	*should be:*
"fife"	"fi<u>v</u>e"
"crass"	"<u>gr</u>ass"

Word Contrasts for Practice

Make sure you pronounce the two words in each pair below differently.

voiceless	voiced
/k/	/g/
1. <u>Cr</u>aig	<u>Gr</u>eg
2. <u>cr</u>ow	<u>gr</u>ow
3. pi<u>ck</u>	pi<u>g</u>
4. ba<u>ck</u>	ba<u>g</u>
/tʃ/	/dʒ/
5. ri<u>ch</u>	ri<u>dge</u>
6. <u>ch</u>oke	<u>j</u>oke
7. bat<u>ch</u>	ba<u>dge</u>
8. <u>ch</u>oice	<u>J</u>oyce
/t/	/d/
9. be<u>t</u>	be<u>d</u>
10. go<u>t</u>	Go<u>d</u>
11. bol<u>t</u>	bol<u>d</u>
12. hear<u>t</u>	har<u>d</u>

	/s/	/z/
13.	pla**c**e	play**s**
14.	pri**c**e	pri**z**e
15.	lo**ss**	law**s**
16.	ra**c**er	ra**z**or
	/f/	/v/
17.	**f**an	**v**an
18.	sa**f**e	sa**v**e
19.	proo**f**	pro**v**e
20.	in**f**est	in**v**est

The *th* Sound

Review Chapters Three and Four to learn the correct pronunciation of this sound. A common mistake is to substitute a /t/ or a /d/ for *th*.

typical mistake:	*should be:*
"tank"	"**th**ank"
"dose"	"**th**ose"
"mudder"	"mo**th**er"

The /n/ Sound

Pay special attention to *n* when it is in the middle or at the end of a word. When the tip of your tongue makes contact with the gum ridge, make sure that you are continuing to produce sound by allowing air to come out through your nose. Otherwise your *n* will be silent.

Words for Practice

1. o**ne**	4. ma**n**	7. **n**i**ne**	10. **n**i**n**etee**n**
2. i**n**vent	5. co**n**vent	8. pro**n**ou**n**ce	11. co**nt**ent
3. fi**n**a**n**cial	6. atte**nti**on	9. me**nti**on	12. co**ns**o**n**a**nt**

Vietnamese speakers also tend to drop the *n* before another consonant. To fix this error, make sure that you fully produce *n* before you begin saying the following consonant. Feel the vibration of air in your nose as the tip of your tongue touches the gum ridge. Common mispronounced words include *understa**nd**, frie**nd**, insta**nt**, importa**nce***, and *se**nse***.

Word Contrasts for Practice
Make sure that you pronounce the two words in each pair below differently.

1. Fre**d**	frie**nd**
2. me**t**	mea**nt**
3. la**d**	la**nd**
4. sa**d**	sa**nd**

Confusing /n/ and /l/

Make sure you do not confuse /n/ and /l/, especially with words like *analysis* or *only* that contain both of these sounds. The primary difference between the two sounds is the location of the air flow. For /n/ the air is coming out through your nose, whereas for /l/ the air is coming out through the sides of your mouth. The tongue position is very similar for these two sounds except the tip of the tongue is a bit flatter for the /n/. For the /l/, the jaw needs to open more to create space for the air to come out through the sides of the mouth. Be careful with words such as *only* and *unless*.

The "r" Sound

Learn to pronounce the correct American /r/ sound by studying Chapter Three and by doing all the /r/ exercises in Chapter Four. Remember, the /r/ is *never* silent in Standard American English, whereas in British English it sometimes is.

typical mistake:	*should be:*
"mo"	"mo**r**e"
"fa"	"fa**r**"
"motha"	"mothe**r**"
"ha"	"he**r**"

Word Pairs for Practice
Make sure you don't pronounce these pairs of words the same:

no *r*	*r*
1. foam	form
2. moaning	morning
3. pot	part
4. tone	torn
5. cone	corn

Consonant Clusters

There's a tendency for Vietnamese speakers to pronounce only the first consonant in a group or cluster. Therefore, *card* can sound like "car" and *extra** can sound like "estra." When there are two or more consonants next to each other, make sure you pronounce *every* consonant. Review the section on consonant clusters in Chapter Four.

one consonant:	two consonants:
"Where's your car?"	"Where's your car**d**?"
"They ask about it."	"They ask**ed** about it."

*Remember, the letter *x* represents two sounds: /ks/

When an *s* is followed by a consonant, make sure you pronounce the /s/. Otherwise the word *sister* will sound like "sitter."

Final Consonants

Make sure you pronounce all of the final sounds of words, particularly those ending in *s*, *v*, *k*, *d*, and *t*.

Vowels

It is recommended that you study all of the American vowel sounds in detail. (See Chapters One and Two.) However, pay special attention to the vowel sounds highlighted below which are the most problematic ones for Vietnamese speakers.

Confusing /æ/ and /ɛ/

The sounds /æ/ (as in *bad*) and /ɛ/ (as in *bed*) are often confused by native Vietnamese speakers. Review Chapters One and Two to master the differences between these two sounds.

Word Contrasts for Practice

Make sure you pronounce the words in each pair below differently.

/æ/	/ɛ/
1. flash	flesh
2. man	men
3. salary	celery
4. ex	axe
5. taxes	Texas
6. sand	send

The /ɔ/ Sound

Be careful that your /ɔ/ sound (as in *saw*) is not influenced by the very different British version of this sound. In British English *pause* sounds almost like "pose," but in American English it sounds much more like /pɑz/, and has the same /ɑ/ sound as in *father* or *watch*.

Word Contrasts for Practice

Don't pronounce the two words in each pair below the same way.

/oʊ/	/ɔ/
1. low	law
2. boat	bought
3. coat	caught
4. woke	walk

The /eɪ/ Sound

Vietnamese speakers commonly pronounce /eɪ/ as /ɛ/ or as /æ/. This makes the pronunciation of *pain*, *pen*, and *pan* all sound the same. Also, *sale* and *sell* will often sound the same when pronounced by a Vietnamese speaker. The words t*a*ke, av*ai*lable, br*ea*k, and f*a*mous are also commonly mispronounced.

Word Contrasts for Practice

Make sure you pronounce the words in each pair below differently.

/ɛ/	/eɪ/
1. sell	sale
2. well	whale
3. tell	tale
4. men	main
5. pen	pain
6. plan	plain

Linking

Vietnamese speakers of English tend to pronounce each word separately, which makes their speech sound choppy and mechanical. The section on linking in Chapter Eight is one of the most important things to study to help you sound more American.

Index